Meditations
for Mortals

Meditations for Mortals

Four Weeks to Embrace
Your Limitations and
Make Time for What
Counts

Oliver Burkeman

 Farrar, Straus and Giroux | New York

Farrar, Straus and Giroux
120 Broadway, New York 10271

Parts of this book have previously appeared in the author's email newsletter,
The Imperfectionist.

Grateful acknowledgment is made to David Cain for permission to
quote from "Care Deeply, Not Passionately," from *Raptitude*; to Virginia
Valian for permission to quote from "Learning to Work"; to Susan Piver
for permission to quote from "Getting Stuff Done by Not Being Mean to
Yourself," from the *Open Heart Project*; and to Jack King for permission
to quote from "Why Scruffy Hospitality Creates Space for Friendship,"
from *KnoxPriest*.
Extract from *The Collected Letters of C. S. Lewis Vol II* by C. S. Lewis
© copyright 2004 C. S. Lewis Pte Ltd. Used with permission.

Library of Congress Control Number: 2024940953
ISBN: 978-0-374-61199-6

Our books may be purchased in bulk for promotional, educational, or
business use. Please contact your local bookseller or the Macmillan
Corporate and Premium Sales Department at 1-800-221-7945,
extension 5442, or by email at MacmillanSpecialMarkets@macmillan.com.

www.fsgbooks.com
Follow us on social media at @fsgbooks

10 9 8 7 6 5 4 3 2 1

'It is easier to try to be better than you are than to be who you are.'

— MARION WOODMAN

'Is there life before death? That is the question!'

— ANTHONY DE MELLO

Contents

Introduction   xv
The imperfect life

Week One   1
BEING FINITE

Day One   3
It's worse than you think
On the liberation of defeat

Day Two   9
Kayaks and superyachts
On actually doing things

Day Three   14
You need only face the consequences
On paying the price

Day Four   20
Against productivity debt
On the power of a 'done list'

Day Five   26
Too much information
On the art of reading and not reading

Day Six   31
You can't care about everything
On staying sane when the world's a mess

Day Seven   37
Let the future be the future
On crossing bridges when you come to them

Week Two   43
TAKING ACTION

Day Eight   45
Decision-hunting
On choosing a path through the woods

Day Nine   51
Finish things
On the magic of completion

Day Ten   55
Look for the life task
On what reality wants

Day Eleven   60
Just go to the shed
On befriending what you fear

Day Twelve   **65**
Rules that serve life
On doing things dailyish

Day Thirteen   **70**
Three hours
On finding focus in the chaos

Day Fourteen   **75**
Develop a taste for problems
On never reaching the trouble-free phase

Week Three   **79**
LETTING GO

Day Fifteen   **81**
What if this were easy?
On the false allure of effort

Day Sixteen   **87**
The reverse golden rule
On not being your own worst enemy

Day Seventeen   **93**
Don't stand in generosity's way
On the futility of 'becoming a better person'

Day Eighteen   **97**
Allow other people their problems
On minding your own business

Day Nineteen   102
A good time or a good story
On the upsides of unpredictability

Day Twenty   108
Set a quantity goal
On firing your inner quality controller

Day Twenty-one   113
What's an interruption, anyway?
On the importance of staying distractible

Week Four   119
SHOWING UP

Day Twenty-two   121
Stop being so kind to Future You
On entering time and space completely

Day Twenty-three   127
How to start from sanity
On paying yourself first

Day Twenty-four   132
Scruffy hospitality
On finding connection in the flaws

Day Twenty-five   138
You can't hoard life
On letting the moments pass

Day Twenty-six   143
Inconceivable
On the solace of doubt

Day Twenty-seven   148
C'est fait par du monde
On giving it a shot

Day Twenty-eight   153
What matters
On finding your way

Epilogue   159
Imperfectly onward

Acknowledgments   163
Further Reading   165
Index of Afflictions   171

Meditations
for Mortals

The imperfect life

This is a book about how the world opens up once you realize you're never going to sort your life out. It's about how marvelously productive you become when you give up the grim-faced quest to make yourself more and more productive; and how much easier it gets to do bold and important things once you accept that you'll never get around to more than a handful of them (and that, strictly speaking, you don't absolutely *need* to do any of them at all). It's about how absorbing, even magical, life becomes when you accept how fleeting and unpredictable it is; how much less isolating it feels to stop hiding your flaws and failures from others; and how liberating it can be to understand that your greatest difficulties in life might never be fully resolved.

In short: it's about what changes once you grasp that life

as a limited human being – in an era of infinite tasks and opportunities, facing an unknowable future, alongside other humans who stubbornly insist on having their own personalities – isn't a problem you've got to try to solve. The twenty-eight chapters in this book are intended as a guide to a different way of taking action in the world, which I call 'imperfectionism' – a freeing and energizing outlook based on the conviction that your limitations aren't *obstacles* to a meaningful existence, which you must spend your days struggling to overcome, en route to some imaginary point when you'll finally get to feel fulfilled. On the contrary, accepting them, stepping more fully into them, is precisely *how* you build a saner, freer, more accomplished, socially connected and enchantment-filled life – and never more so than at this volatile and anxiety-inducing moment in history.

If you decide to read this book at the suggested pace of one chapter per day or thereabouts, my hope is that it will function as a four-week 'retreat of the mind' in the midst of daily life – a way of actually living this philosophy here and now, and doing more of what matters to you as a result, instead of mentally filing it away as yet another system you might try to implement one day, should you ever get a moment to spare. After all, as we'll see, one main tenet of imperfectionism is that the day is never coming when all the other stuff will be 'out of the way,' so you can turn at last to building a life of meaning and accomplishment that hums with vitality. For finite humans, the time for that has to be now.

So I sincerely hope you find this book useful. To be completely honest with you, though, I wrote it for myself.

In my late twenties, I started working as a general feature writer at the *Guardian* newspaper in London, where my job, upon arriving at the office in the morning, was to be assigned some topic currently in the news – the fate of refugees fleeing an unfolding geopolitical crisis, say, or why green smoothies were suddenly so popular – and then to turn in a big-picture, intelligent-seeming 2,000-word article on it by 5 p.m. the same day. An hour or two before deadline, my editor would begin pacing the floor near my desk, clicking his fingers to expel nervous energy, and wondering aloud why I wasn't closer to finishing. The answer (as I doubtless told him on several occasions) is that writing an intelligent-seeming 2,000-word article in seven hours flat, on a topic about which you previously knew nothing, is a fundamentally preposterous undertaking. Still, it had to be done – and so my days at the *Guardian* were shot through with the feeling of being on the back foot, fighting against time, and needing to buckle down immediately, if I were to stand any chance of closing the gap.

Not that I can really blame my editor for any of this. By that point in my life, I was already on intimate terms with the feeling of playing catch-up; indeed, few things feel more basic to my experience of adulthood than the vague sense that I'm falling behind, and need to claw my way back up to a minimum standard of output, if I'm to stave off an ill-defined catastrophe that might otherwise come crashing down upon my head. Sometimes, it felt like all I needed was a bit more discipline; at other times, I was sure the answer lay in a new system for managing my tasks and goals, which I'd track down just as soon as I got this article on smoothies out of the way. I devoured self-help books, tried meditation, and explored Stoicism, growing slightly more anxious each time another new technique proved not to be the silver bullet. Always over the horizon, meanwhile, hovered the fantasy of one day 'getting on top of things' – where 'things' could mean anything from emptying my inbox to figuring out how romantic relationships were supposed to work – so that the truly meaningful part of life, the really *real* part, could finally begin.

I know now, though I didn't back then, that I'm not alone in feeling this way. Frankly, I could hardly be less alone. Hundreds of conversations and email exchanges I've had since 2021, when I published a book about the challenge of using time well, have convinced me that this sense of not having life nailed down just yet – and needing to exert one-self harder and harder, if only to avoid slipping further back – is close to universal these days. The younger people I encountered seemed utterly daunted by the task of getting life into working order, while many older ones were dismayed that by forty or fifty they apparently still hadn't managed it, and were starting to wonder if they ever would. Certainly, it was clear that achieving wealth or status didn't cause the problem to go away – which makes sense, since in the modern world, external success is often the result of being even more enmeshed in the desperate game of catch-up than everyone else. 'Most successful people,' as the entrepreneur and investor

Andrew Wilkinson has observed, 'are just a walking anxiety disorder, harnessed for productivity.'

The most common form of the anxious feeling I'm trying to pinpoint here is sheer, overwhelming busyness, the sense of having far too much to do in the time available for doing it. But it takes other forms as well. For some it manifests as imposter syndrome, the belief that there's a basic level of expertise that pretty much everyone else has attained, but that you haven't, and that you won't be able to stop second-guessing yourself until you get there. It also arises, for many of us, in the feeling of not yet having cracked the code of intimate relationships, so that for all our outward accomplishments we feel thwarted on a daily basis by the bewildering complexities of dating, marriage, or parenting. For still others, the falling-behind feeling is mainly a matter of believing they ought to be doing more to address the national and global crises unfolding around them, but having no idea what they could do, as individuals, that could possibly make any difference. The thread that runs through all these, though, is the idea that there exists some way of being in the world, some way of *mastering the situation* of being a human in the twenty-first century, that you have yet to discover. And that you won't be able to relax into your life until you do.

Yet the worst of it is that our efforts to address the problem seem only to exacerbate it. In my book *Four Thousand Weeks* I labeled one version of this 'the efficiency trap,' to describe the way that when you get better and faster at dealing with an incoming supply of anything, you often end up busier and more stressed. Email is the classic example:

vowing to address the deluge, you start replying more promptly, triggering more replies, many of which you'll need to reply to; plus, you acquire a reputation for being unusually responsive on email, so more people consider it worthwhile to email you in the first place. Moreover, as you struggle to handle everything, your days begin to fill with less important tasks – because your belief that there must be a way to do it all means you flinch from making difficult decisions about what's truly worth your limited time.

But my conversations helped me recognize a deeper issue, too, which is the way our ceaseless efforts to get into the driver's seat of life seem to sap it of the very sense of aliveness that makes it worth living in the first place. The days lose what the German social theorist Hartmut Rosa evocatively calls their 'resonance.' The world feels dead; and for all our efforts to get more done, we find ourselves somehow less able to bring about the results we were seeking. It happens even when our attempts to get in control of things *do* work. You manage to make yourself meditate daily, and suddenly it feels soul-crushingly boring to do so; or you get around to organizing a date night with your spouse – because everyone says that's how to keep the spark alive – but the whole thing makes the two of you so self-conscious that it's fated to descend into bickering, and you end the evening feeling like failures. In my days as a 'productivity geek,' I was always embracing some new system for designing my life, and as I downloaded the relevant app, or purchased the required stationery, I'd feel excited, even intoxicated: I was on the verge of great things! Then, within a day or two, my new schedule would seem dismal and lifeless, another list of chores I had to slog through, and I'd find myself angrily resenting the jerk who had the temerity to dictate how I spent my time in this manner – even though the jerk in question was me.

These are admittedly minor examples. But this loss of aliveness also helps explain the epidemic of burnout, which isn't merely a matter of exhaustion, but of the emptiness that comes from years of pushing oneself, machine-like, to do more and more, without it ever feeling like enough. The increasingly rage-filled and conspiratorial character of modern political life might even be seen as a desperate attempt, by people starved of resonance, to try to feel anything at all.

The essential trouble, as Rosa tells it, is that the driving force of modern life is the fatally misguided idea that reality can and should be made ever more controllable – and that peace of mind and prosperity lie in bringing it ever more fully under our control. And so we experience the world as an endless series of things we must master, learn, or conquer. We set out to make mincemeat of our inboxes, defeat our to-read piles, or impose order on our schedules; we try to optimize our levels of fitness or focus, and feel obliged to be always enhancing our parenting skills, competence in personal finance, or understanding of world events. (Even if we congratulate ourselves on, say, prioritizing friendship over making money, we may still approach it in the spirit of optimization, pushing ourselves to make more friends, or to do better at keeping in touch with them – that is, to try to exert more control over our social lives.) The culture reinforces this doctrine of control in multiple ways. Advances in technology always seem on the cusp of permitting you to tame your workload at last – at the time of writing, virtual assistants powered by artificial intelligence are what's about to do it – while the hyper-competitive economy makes it feel ever more essential to do so, just to keep your head above water.

Yet everyday experience, along with centuries of philosophical reflection, attests to the fact that a fulfilling and accomplished life *isn't* a matter of exerting ever more control. It's not about making things more predictable and secure, until you can finally relax. A football match is exciting because you *don't* know who'll win; a field of intellectual study is absorbing because you *don't* yet have a handle on it all. The greatest achievements often involve remaining open to serendipity, seizing unplanned opportunities, or riding unexpected bursts of motivation. To be delighted by another person, or moved by a landscape or a work of art, requires not being in full control. At the same time, a good life clearly isn't about giving up all hope of influencing reality. It's about taking bold action, creating things, and making an impact – just without the background agenda of achieving full control. Resonance depends on reciprocity: you do things – you have to launch the business, organize the campaign, set off on the wilderness trek, send the email about the social event – and then see how the world responds.

It's hardly surprising that so many of us spend so much of our lives attempting to lever ourselves into a position of dominance over a reality that can otherwise seem so unmanageable and overwhelming. How else are you supposed to handle all those to-dos, pursue a few cherished ambitions, take a stab at being a decent parent or partner, and do your bit as a citizen of a world in crisis? But it doesn't work. Life edges ever closer to being a dull, solitary, and often infuriating chore, something to be endured, in order to make it to a supposedly better time, which never quite seems to arrive.

Meditations for Mortals is my attempt to begin where the sort-your-life-out, get-on-top-of-everything school of thinking fails, and instead go somewhere more meaningful and productive, and importantly also more fun. (The chapters draw heavily on my email newsletter *The Imperfectionist*, and on many generous responses from its readers.) Rather than fueling the fantasy of one day bringing everything under control, this book takes it as a given that you'll *never* get on top of everything. It starts from the position that you'll never feel fully confident about the future, or fully understand what makes other people tick – and that there will always be too much to do.

But none of this is because you're an ill-disciplined loser, or because you haven't yet read the right bestseller revealing 'the surprising science' of productivity, leadership, parenting, or anything else. It's because being a finite human *just means* never achieving the sort of control or security on which many of us feel our sanity depends. It just means that the list of worthwhile things you could in principle do with your time will always be vastly longer than the list of things for which you'll have time. It just means you'll always be vulnerable to unforeseen disasters or distressing emotions, and that you'll never have more than partial influence over how your time unfolds, no matter what YouTubers in their early twenties with no kids might have to say about the ideal morning routine.

Imperfectionism is the outlook that understands this to be good news. It's not that facing finitude isn't painful. (That's why the quest for control is so alluring.) Confronting your non-negotiable limitations means accepting that life entails tough choices and sacrifices, that regret is always a possibility, as is disappointing others, and that nothing you create in the world will ever measure up to the perfect standards in your head. But these truths are also the very things that liberate you to act, and to experience resonance. When you give up the unwinnable struggle to do everything, that's when you can start pouring your finite time and attention into a handful of things that truly count. When you no longer demand perfection from your creative work, your relationships, or anything else, that's when you're free to plunge energetically into them. And when you stop making your sanity or self-worth dependent on first reaching a state of control that humans don't get to experience, you're able to start feeling sane and enjoying life now, which is the only time it ever is.

This volume also tries to address a problem that's gnawed at me for years about books purporting to help people live more meaningfully or productively. The worst of these just offer a list of steps to implement – which almost never works, since they ignore the internal journey the author had to take in order to arrive at them. (If *they* had to struggle with, say, the emotional roots of their resistance to getting organized, why should *you* expect results from merely following a list of organizational tips?) A better sort of book offers a shift in perspective, a changed understanding from which different actions can follow. But shifts in perspective fade depressingly quickly: for a few days, everything seems different; but then the overwhelming momentum of the usual way of doing things reasserts itself once more.

So my goal here is for whatever you might find useful in these pages to sink under your skin and into your bones – and thus to persist. Obviously, how you read this book is among countless aspects of reality I can't possibly hope to control, and it can absolutely be approached like any other. But I invite you to proceed at one chapter per day, in order, through four weeks that have been designed to build on each other: facing the facts of finitude in Week One; taking bold, imperfect action in Week Two; getting out of your own way and letting action happen in Week Three; and finally, in Week Four, showing up more fully for life in the present, rather than later.

In describing this as a 'retreat of the mind,' I mean to suggest that you approach it as a return, on a roughly daily basis, to a metaphorical sanctuary in a quiet corner of your brain, where you can allow new thinking to take shape without needing to press pause on the rest of your life, but which remains there in the background as you go through the day. The chapters feature both shifts in perspective and practical techniques, and my hope is that sometimes one of them will change, in a small but concrete way, how you live through the twenty-four hours after reading it. *That's* what makes change last, in my experience: real feedback, from doing things differently in real life.

Naturally, if *Meditations for Mortals* works on these terms, I can only expect it to do so imperfectly. Relatedly, I recommend making no over-industrious efforts to retain what you read, or to put it into practice; instead, trust that if something strikes a chord, it'll linger through the day by itself. This isn't one of those books promising that if you implement its contents flawlessly, you'll have the ideal system for running your life. Human finitude ensures that's never coming. Which is exactly the reason to dive wholeheartedly into this life, now.

Week One

Being Finite

'If you find yourself lost in the woods, fuck it, build a house. "Well, I was lost, but now I live here! I have severely improved my predicament!"'

— MITCH HEDBERG

DAY ONE

It's worse than you think
On the liberation of defeat

'What is true is already so. Owning up to it doesn't
make it worse. Not being open about it doesn't make it
go away. And because it's true, it is what is there to be
interacted with. Anything untrue isn't there to be
lived. People can stand what is true, for they are
already enduring it.'

— EUGENE GENDLIN

T he most liberating and empowering and productive
step you can take, if you want to spend more of your
time on the planet doing what matters to you, is to
grasp the sense in which life as a finite human being – with
limited time, and limited control over that time – is really
much worse than you think. Completely beyond hope, in
fact. You know that cloud of melancholy that sometimes

3

descends – when you're awake in the dark at three in the morning, perhaps, or towards the end of a frazzled Thursday at work – when it seems as though the life you'd envisaged for yourself might never come to fruition after all? The magic begins when you understand that it *definitely* won't come to fruition.

It is true that I have been accused of being a killjoy. So I should probably try to explain why this isn't depressing at all.

Consider – just to begin with – the familiar modern predicament of feeling overwhelmed by an extremely long to-do list. You *think* the problem is that you have far too many things to do, and insufficient time in which to do them, so that your only hope is to manage your time with amazing efficiency, summon extraordinary reserves of energy, block out all distractions, and somehow power through to the end. In fact, your situation is worse than you think – because the truth is that the incoming supply of things that feel as though they genuinely need doing isn't merely large, but to all intents and purposes infinite. So getting through them all isn't just very difficult. It's impossible.

But this is where things get interesting, because an important psychological shift occurs whenever you realize that a struggle you'd been approaching as if it were very difficult is actually completely impossible. Something inside unclenches. It's equivalent to that moment when, caught in a rainstorm without an umbrella, you finally abandon your futile efforts to stay dry, and accept getting soaked to the skin. *Very well, then: this is how things are.* Once you see it's just unavoidably the case that you'll only ever get to do a fraction of the things that in an ideal world you might like to do, anxiety subsides, and a new willingness arises to get stuck in to what you actually can do. It's not that life becomes instantly effortless: depending on your situation, there might be serious repercussions to letting certain tasks fall by the wayside. But if doing everything that's demanded of you, or that you're demanding of yourself, is genuinely impossible, then, well, it's impossible, and facing the truth can only help. After that – once you're staring reality in the face – you can take action not in the tense hope that your actions might be leading you towards some future utopia of perfect productivity, but simply because they're worth doing.

Busyness might not be a major problem for you, of course. Your problem might be that you're a perfectionist, who suffers anguish in your efforts to produce work that meets your exacting standards. But that situation's worse than you think, too, because the truth is that no work you bring into concrete existence could ever meet the perfect standards in your mind. Imposter syndrome? You might believe you need more experience or qualifications in order to feel confident among your peers; but the truth is that even the most experienced and qualified people feel as though they're winging it, much of the time – and that if you're ever going to make your unique contribution to the world, you'll probably have to do it in a state of feeling unprepared. Relationship troubles? They're worse than you think, as well. Maybe it's true that you married the wrong person, or that you need years of therapy – yet it's also just a fact that two flawed and finite humans, living and maturing together, will inevitably push each other's buttons, triggering their buried issues. (It's the ones who claim never to have experienced anything of the sort that you should wonder about.)

The late British Zen master Hōun Jiyu-Kennett, born Peggy Kennett, had a vivid way of capturing the sense of inner release that can come from grasping just how intractable our human limitations really are. Her teaching style, she liked to say, was not to lighten the burden of the student, but to make it so heavy that he or she would put it down. Metaphorically speaking, lightening someone's burden means encouraging them to believe that, with sufficient effort, their struggles might be overcome: that they might indeed find a way to feel like they're doing enough, or that they're competent enough, or that relationships are a piece of cake, and so on. Kennett's insight was that it can often be kinder and more effective to make their burden heavier – to help them see how totally irredeemable their situation is, thereby giving them permission to stop struggling.

And then? Then you get to relax. But you also get to accomplish more, and to enjoy yourself more in the process, because you're no longer so busy denying the reality of your predicament, consciously or otherwise. This is the point at which you enter the sacred state the writer Sasha Chapin refers to as 'playing in the ruins.'

In his twenties, Chapin recalls, his definition of a successful life was that he should become a celebrated novelist, on a par with David Foster Wallace. When that didn't happen – when his perfectionistic fantasies ran up against his real-world limitations – he found it unexpectedly liberating. The failure he'd told himself he couldn't possibly allow to occur had, in fact, occurred, and it hadn't destroyed him.

Now he was free to be the writer he actually could be. When this sort of confrontation with limitation takes place, Chapin writes, 'a precious state of being can dawn ... You're not seeing the landscape around you as something that needs to transform. You're just seeing it as the scrapyard it is. And then you can look around yourself and say, okay, what is actually here, when I'm not telling myself constant lies about what it's going to be one day?' With this comes the bracing understanding that you might as well get on with life: that it's precisely *because* you'll never produce perfect work that you might as well get on with doing the best work you can; and that it's *because* intimate relationships are too complex ever to be negotiated entirely smoothly that you might as well commit to one, and see what happens. There are no guarantees – except the guarantee that holding back from life instead is a recipe for anguish.

Because our problem, it turns out, was never that we hadn't yet found the right way to achieve control *over* life, or safety *from* life. Our real problem was imagining that any of that might be possible in the first place for finite humans, who, after all, just find themselves unavoidably *in* life, with all the limitations and feelings of claustrophobia and lack of escape routes that entails. ('Our suffering,' as Mel Weitsman, another Zen teacher, puts it, 'is believing there's a way out.') When you grasp the sense in which your situation is worse than you thought, you no longer have to go through life adopting the brace position, desperately hoping someone will find a way to prevent the plane from crashing. You understand that the plane has already crashed. (It crashed, for you, the moment you were born.) You're already stranded on the desert island, with nothing but old airplane food to subsist on, and no option but to make the best of life with your fellow survivors.

Very well, then: here you are. Here we all are. Now ... what might be some good things to do with your time?

Kayaks and superyachts

On actually doing things

'That which seems like a false step is just the next step.'

— AGNES MARTIN

At this point in a book on getting around to what counts, you might be expecting some kind of a *system*.

That was how it always went with me, anyway. On picking up a work that made any kind of promise about building a more successful or meaningful life, I'd immediately flick past the opening pages to the part where the author set out his or her step-by-step system for actually making it happen. Few things are more appealing, when you're hoping to change your life, than a new system for doing so. But that allure can lead you astray. Almost nobody wants to hear the real answer to the question of how to spend more of your finite time doing things that matter to you, which involves no system. The answer is: you just do them. You pick something you genuinely care about, and then, for at least a few minutes – a quarter of an hour, say – you do some of it. Today. It really is that simple. Unfortunately, for many of us, it also turns out to be one of the hardest things in the world.

It's not that systems for getting things done are *bad*, exactly. (Rules for meaningful productivity do have a role to play, and we'll turn to some of them later.) It's just that they're not the main point. The main point – though it took me years to realize it – is to develop the willingness to just do something, here and now, as a one-off, regardless of whether it's part of any system or habit or routine. If you don't prioritize the skill of just doing something, you risk falling into an exceedingly sneaky trap, which is that you end up embarking instead on the unnecessary and, worse, counterproductive project of *becoming the kind of person who does that sort of thing*.

The problem I'm referring to arises like this: you want the peace and clarity you believe you'd derive from meditation, say, so you resolve to become a meditator. You purchase a book on changing your habits, skim through it, then start figuring out how best to make a meditation habit stick. You order a meditation cushion. Perhaps you even get as far as sitting down to meditate. But then something goes wrong. Maybe the sheer scale of the project of 'becoming a meditator' – that is, meditating day after day for the rest of your life – strikes you as daunting, so you decide to postpone the whole affair to some point in the future, when you expect to have more energy and time. Alternatively, maybe the novelty of becoming a meditator positively thrills you – until a week or two later, when monotony sets in, and the letdown feels so intolerable that you throw in the towel.

What you could have done instead was to forget about the whole project of 'becoming a meditator,' and focus solely on sitting down to meditate. Once. For five minutes.

It's worth mentioning another version of this problem, in which people try to become a different kind of person as a way to unconsciously avoid doing the activity in question. Suppose you want to start a business, but the prospect intimidates you. What better way to never quite get around to it than to turn it into a long-term project? That way, you get to spend months doing research, and undertaking brainstorming exercises, and emulating the daily routine of one of your entrepreneurial idols, complete with 5 a.m. wake-ups and a 'hydration protocol' ... and you never have to do the scary thing at all.

A pair of images that help clarify things here are those of the kayak and the superyacht. To be human, according to this analogy, is to occupy a little one-person kayak, borne along on the river of time towards your inevitable yet unpredictable death. It's a thrilling situation, but also an intensely vulnerable one: you're at the mercy of the current, and all you can really do is to stay alert, steering as best you can, reacting as wisely and gracefully as possible to whatever arises from moment to moment. The German philosopher Martin Heidegger described this state of affairs using the word *Geworfenheit*, or 'thrownness,' a suitably awkward word for an awkward predicament: merely to come into existence is to find oneself thrown into a time and place you didn't choose, with a personality you didn't pick, and with your time flowing away beneath you, minute by minute, whether you like it or not.

That's how life *is*. But it isn't how we want it to be. We'd prefer a much greater sense of control. Rather than paddling by kayak, we'd like to feel ourselves the captain of a super-yacht, calm and in charge, programming our desired route into the ship's computers, then sitting back and watching it all unfold from the plush-leather swivel chair on the serene and silent bridge. Systems and schemes for self-improvement, and 'long-term projects,' all feed this fantasy: you get to spend your time daydreaming that you're on the superyacht, master of all you survey, and imagining how great it'll feel to reach your destination. By contrast, actually doing one mean-ingful thing today – just sitting down to meditate, just writing a few paragraphs of the novel, just giving your full attention to one exchange with your child – requires surren-dering a sense of control. It means not knowing in advance if you'll carry it off well (you can be certain you'll do it imper-fectly), or whether you'll end up becoming the kind of person who does that sort of thing all the time. And so it is an act of faith. It means facing the truth that you're always in the kayak, never the superyacht.

The challenge, then, is simple, though for many of us also excruciating: What's one thing you could do today – or tomorrow at the latest, if you're reading this at night – that would constitute a good-enough use of a chunk of your finite time, and that you'd actually be willing to do? (Don't get dis-tracted wondering what might be the *best* thing to do: that's superyacht thinking, borne of the desire to feel certain you're on the right path.) Because the irony, of course, is that just doing something once today, just steering your kayak over the next few inches of water, is the only way you'll ever become the kind of person who does that sort of thing on a regular basis anyway. Otherwise – and believe me, I've been there – you're merely the kind of person who spends your life drawing up plans for how you're going to become a different kind of person later on. This will sometimes garner you the admiration of others, since it can look from the outside like you're busily making improvements. But it isn't the same at all.

So you just do the thing, once, with absolutely no guarantee you'll ever manage to do it again. But then perhaps you find that you *do* do it again, the next day, or a few days later, and maybe again, and again – until before you know it, you've developed that most remarkable thing, not a willpower-driven system or routine but an emergent *practice* of writing, or meditating, or listening to your kids, or building a business. Something you do not solely to become a better sort of person – though it may have that effect, too – but because whatever you're bringing into reality, right here on the rapids, is worth bringing into reality for itself.

You need only face the consequences

On paying the price

'You are free to do whatever you like. You need only face the consequences.'

— SHELDON B. KOPP

A friend of mine was trying to decide whether to leave his marriage. Through neither partner's fault, it was clearly headed nowhere good, but he felt paralyzed by two equally appalling options. To walk away would mean causing anguish to his wife, and scandalizing his traditionalist family; but to grit his teeth and stay would be to condemn both of them to decades of misery, or force his wife to do the leaving. As it's all too easy to do in such dilemmas, he'd subconsciously concluded that if a given option wouldn't be painless – and it was clear that neither option would be – it must therefore be impossible. So he froze in place, hoping some third option might magically make itself known.

It took a while before it dawned on him that there was a different way to approach the situation: not a third option, but a new perspective on the existing ones. He saw that he could acknowledge that leaving would be terrible, yet that if it mattered to him enough, he was free to do it anyway, and to deal as responsibly as he could with the resulting awfulness as the price he was willing to pay. Facing this truth – that the choice would come with costs, and that he could elect to shoulder them – gave him the psychological room for maneuver he'd been missing. He left. It *was* awful. But life moved on.

At some point, as you seek to spend more of your finite existence in the ways that feel most meaningful to you, the thought will inevitably occur to you that you *can't* make a certain choice about your time, however much you'd like to, because the circumstances simply don't allow it. The obstacle could be as weighty as the belief that you can't walk away from a marriage or a dispiriting career, because of the emotional or financial impact on yourself or on others. Or it might be as mundane as the notion that you can't spend half an hour on an exhilarating creative project today, because there are too many emails to be answered, or too many household chores that need completing first. These are valid concerns. But the idea that they eliminate all room for choice isn't entirely correct. The truth, though it often makes people indignant to hear it, is that it's almost never literally the case that you *have to* meet a work deadline, honor a commitment, answer an email, fulfill a family obligation, or anything else. The astounding reality – in the words of Sheldon B. Kopp, a genial and brilliant American psychotherapist who died in 1999 – is that you're pretty much free to do whatever you like. You need only face the consequences.

Consequences aren't optional. It's in the nature of being finite that every choice comes with some sort of consequences, because at any instant, you can only pick one path, and must deal with the repercussions of not picking any of the others. Spending a week's holiday in Rome means not spending that same week in Paris; avoiding a conflict in the short term means dealing with whatever might result from letting a bad situation fester. Freedom isn't a matter of somehow wriggling free of the costs of your choice – that's never an option – but of realizing, as Kopp points out, that nothing stops you doing anything at all, so long as you're willing to pay those costs. Unless you're literally being physically coerced into doing something, the notion that you 'have to do it' in truth means that you've chosen not to pay the price of refusing; just as the notion that you absolutely can't do something generally means you're unwilling to pay the price of doing it. You *could* quit your job with no backup plan. You *could* book a one-way ticket to Rio de Janeiro, or rob a bank, or tell your social media followers your honest views. The conservative American economist Thomas Sowell summed things up with a bleakness I appreciate, insisting that there are no solutions, only trade-offs. The only two questions, at any moment of choice in life, is what the price is, and whether or not it's worth paying.

This can come as a revelation and a liberation to the

anxious among us – partly because it cuts genuinely agonizing choices down to a more manageable number, but also because it reminds us that most of the potential consequences we find ourselves agonizing about don't remotely justify such angst. If ignoring an email causes its sender a flicker of irritation, or if your in-laws frown at your approach to parenting, the correct response might very well be: So what? Laura Vanderkam, who has interviewed many working mothers for books on how to manage work and family life, frequently hears versions of the same refrain: 'I can't relax in the evening until the children's toys are tidied away!' But the reality, of course, is that you absolutely *can* relax with the toys not tidied away. 'There is no 11 p.m. home inspection, with someone coming round to see if all the toys are picked up,' notes Vanderkam. You need only be willing to pay the price of relaxing in such circumstances, which is a less-than-pristine home.

There's an elephant in the room here that can't be tidied away, of course, which is that the consequences of any given choice might be vastly more severe for some people than for others. There are those who'd get fired if they ignored a few emails, or violently abused for a toy-strewn house. But these grossly unfair realities don't change the fact that each choice is always and only a matter of weighing the trade-offs. If a path you'd love to take is genuinely likely to leave you destitute, or seriously harmed in some other way, then you probably shouldn't take it. But for most of us, if we're being honest with ourselves, the temptation is often to exaggerate potential consequences, so as to spare ourselves the burden of making a bold choice. (It's a particular peril among the progressive-minded, I've noticed, to take the fact that a given choice might be unfeasible for the underprivileged as a reason not to make it yourself. But unless it's *you* who's underprivileged, that's an alibi, not an argument.) It was a central insight of the philosopher Jean-Paul Sartre that there's a secret comfort in telling yourself you've got no options, because it's easier to wallow in the 'bad faith' of believing yourself trapped than to face the dizzying responsibilities of your freedom.

But the liberation can be dizzying, too. When you begin approaching life as a matter of facing consequences, you'll frequently find yourself declining to spend time on things you never much cared for in the first place, but might previously not have dared turn down. (Some people are naturals at this: 'Oh dear,' the English comedian Peter Cook is said to have responded when David Frost, the journalist and chat-show host, phoned to invite him to dinner with Prince Andrew and his then wife, Sarah Ferguson. 'Checking my diary, I find I'm watching television that night.') At other times, though, you'll go ahead and do the undesired thing anyway, because you understand the cost and you *don't* want to incur it. Notice how different that is – how different it feels – from grudgingly saying yes because you 'feel you have no choice,' then resenting it for days. For example, perhaps you care enough about the friend who's asking you to cancel your plans and help her move house this weekend that it's worth saying yes: the stress and disappointment you'd cause her by refusing is a price you're unwilling to pay.

Whatever choice you make, so long as you make it in the spirit of facing the consequences, the result will be freedom in the only sense that finite humans ever get to enjoy it.

Not freedom *from* limitation, which is something we unfortunately never get to experience, but freedom *in* limitation. Freedom to examine the trade-offs – because there will always be trade-offs – and then to opt for whichever trade-off you like.

Against productivity debt

On the power of a 'done list'

'One never notices what has been done; one can see only what remains to be done.'

— MARIE CURIE

L et's pause here to remember that you don't actually have to do any of this. Use your time in a worthwhile manner, I mean. Find ways to get around to what matters most. None of it's compulsory. You have my permission not to bother.

Many people these days report the feeling that they begin each morning in a kind of 'productivity debt,' which they must struggle to pay off over the course of the day, in hopes of returning to a zero balance by the time evening comes. If they fail – or worse, don't even try – it's as though they haven't quite justified their existence on the planet. If this describes you, there's a good chance that like me you belong to the gloomy bunch psychologists label 'insecure overachievers,' which is a diplomatic way of saying that our accomplishments, impressive as they may sometimes be, are driven ultimately by feelings of inadequacy. For example, maybe you believe that you'll have earned your right to exist only when you attain a certain level of social standing, or income, or academic qualifications. Or perhaps you've tethered your self-esteem to the most crazy-making standard of all, 'realizing your potential' – which means you'll never get to rest, because how can you ever be sure there's not a little more potential left to realize?

The truth is that you don't need to do any of this.

Of course, there's a mundane sense in which we 'need' to do all sorts of things: in order to pay the rent, you must generate an income; if you do that by working at a job, you'd better meet your employer's requirements, or you can expect to run into trouble. If you have kids, it's generally a good idea to provide them with food and clothing. But we overlay this everyday sense of obligation with the existential duty described above: the feeling that we need to get things done not only to achieve certain ends, or to meet our basic responsibilities to others, but because it's a cosmic debt we've somehow incurred in exchange for being alive. As the philosopher Byung-Chul Han has written, 'we produce against the feeling of lack.' Our frenetic activity is often an effort to shore up a sense of ourselves as minimally acceptable members of society.

Where all these feelings of inadequacy come from is debatable and complex. You could start by blaming the Protestant work ethic, the ideology that took root in early modern Europe whereby Calvinist Christians came to believe that unflagging hard work might demonstrate their suitability for entering heaven after they died. (It wasn't that hard work would *gain* them a place there, since they believed that everyone's fate was predestined; theirs was the much more psychologically complicated position that if they'd already been selected for heaven, they should expect themselves to be the kind of people who'd naturally want to work hard anyway.) You can probably blame your parents, too, who can blame theirs in turn, since research suggests that many 'insecure overachievers' start off as children raised to feel noticed and valued only when they're excelling at things. Oh, and you can also blame consumerism, which has an obvious vested interest in keeping people feeling inadequate, so they might be relied upon to purchase goods and services that promise to make the feelings go away.

What's not debatable, though, is that life as a productivity debtor is no fun at all. It's anxiety-inducing, and exhausting, and it probably also contributes to the modern epidemic of social isolation, since a tunnel-vision focus on paying off your debt makes it much less appealing to prioritize apparently unproductive activities like hanging out with your friends. Worse still, the productivity-debt mindset turns success into a kind of punishment: each new accomplishment merely sets a higher standard that you now feel you've got to reach next time around, so it becomes even harder to pay off your debt than it was before.

This must be why it comes as such a punch to the guts whenever I revisit a scene from the largely forgotten noughties television drama *Studio 60 on the Sunset Strip*, in which Bradley Whitford and the late Matthew Perry play producers called in to rescue and relaunch a national weekly comedy show, based transparently on *Saturday Night Live*. Throughout the episode, their anxiety builds visibly, while a huge digital clock on the control-room wall counts down the days, hours, minutes and seconds until the moment the live broadcast must begin. The world is watching. The stakes are high. Last-minute conflicts threaten to derail the whole thing. But against the odds, as the digits tick down to zero, they manage it. *On air*. The opening song is a knockout. The audience goes wild. The scene cuts to Perry, watching from the back; for the first time, he looks relaxed. For a second or two. Then a troubling thought strikes him, and the camera follows his gaze to the clock on the wall, which now shows 6 days, 23 hours, 57 minutes and 53 seconds: the countdown to next week's broadcast. His reward for paying off his debt so spectacularly is that now he's got to do it, just as impressively, *all over again*.

There is a religious route out of productivity debt, if you believe in a god who bestows grace – who loves you and delights in you, in other words, regardless of how hard you strive to justify your existence by means of your productivity, goodness, or anything else. But agnostics and atheists get to take a different path to a similar destination: if there isn't a god, then there's no authority with the power to demand that you earn your right to exist. You just do exist, and that has to be sufficient. As the Taoist writer Jason Gregory explains, expressing the same idea in a different and powerful way, we fall into the error of believing that we somehow don't belong to the world, and must therefore spend our lives trying to earn back the right to belong. But who could ever decide we don't belong? The obvious truth is that we already do. This isn't sentimentalism, just a hard-nosed statement of the facts. Look around: this is reality. It consists of a whole lot of atoms, a few of which constitute you. What could it even *mean* to say you don't belong?

My favorite way of combating the feeling of productivity debt in everyday life is to keep a 'done list,' which you use to create a record not of the tasks you plan to carry out, but of the ones you've completed so far today – which makes it the rare kind of list that's actually supposed to get longer as the day goes on. (If you already use some kind of task-management system, creating a done list might be as simple as just not deleting tasks once you've finished them, but moving them instead to a separate file or folder, where you can watch with satisfaction as they accumulate.) As Marie Curie understood, our default stance is to measure our actual accomplishments against all the things we could, in principle, still do. But that's a yardstick against which we're doomed to find ourselves perpetually wanting. By contrast, what makes a done list so motivating and encouraging is that it implicitly invites you to compare your output to the hypothetical situation in which you stayed in bed and did nothing at all. And what makes that comparison any less legitimate than the other one? (Plus, if you're really stuck in a rut, you can always define more loosely what gets to count as a completed task. Nobody else ever needs to know you added 'made coffee' or 'took a shower' to your done list.)

A done list isn't solely a way to feel better about yourself, though. When you start to view each day not as a matter of paying off a debt, but as an opportunity to move a small-but-meaningful number of items over to your done list, you'll find yourself making better choices about what to focus on; and you'll make more progress on them, too, since you'll be wasting less energy stressing about all the other tasks you're (inevitably) neglecting. And while I'm not going to pretend it happens all the time, you might even experience a few of those transcendent moments in which taking action on a project you care about – now that it's no longer serving the hidden agenda of making you feel better about yourself by helping you repay an imaginary debt – becomes utterly effortless and joyful.

This is the lesson we insecure overachievers could do with getting into our skulls: actions don't have to be things that we grind out, day after day, in order to inch ever closer to some elusive state of finally getting to qualify as adequate humans. Instead, they can just be enjoyable expressions of the fact that that's what we already are.

Too much information

On the art of reading and not reading

'People today are in danger of drowning in information; but, because they have been taught that information is useful, they are more willing to drown than they need be.'

— IDRIES SHAH

A t the *Guardian*, the topic on which my colleagues and I were most frequently asked to write lifestyle features was 'information overload' – and no, the irony wasn't lost on us that publishing thousands of words on the problem was hardly going to help. This was the mid-2000s, but it was already obvious that the internet was going to exponentially exacerbate the problem of there being far too much to read. (By 1999, researchers estimated, the quantity of data generated worldwide came to at least 1.5 billion gigabytes. The 2024 estimate is 147 trillion gigabytes. Much of it isn't in the form of published content, of course, but plenty is – and by comparison, according to one amateur back-of-the-envelope calculation, the entire Library of Alexandria contained around 12 gigabytes.) It's become a ubiquitous modern problem to have not only a teetering pile of books you've been meaning to read, but a digital stack of articles you'd like to digest, plus a long queue of podcast episodes to listen to, videos or TV shows to watch, or video-games you've purchased and would love to play, if only you could find the time.

It's grimly amusing to reflect that at an earlier stage in the history of the internet, information overload was widely held to be a temporary problem. Yes, for the time being we were being deluged with a zillion irrelevant blog posts, emails and news updates. But it wouldn't last, because soon there'd be better technology to help us find the information we really valued, while disregarding the rest. The real trouble, according to the prominent techno-optimist Clay Shirky, wasn't information overload but 'filter failure.' All we really needed – and would presumably imminently get – were more sophisticated ways to filter the digital wheat from the chaff.

It didn't exactly work out that way. What happened, instead, was a textbook case of the 'efficiency trap.' It's true that the filters got much better: technologies such as Amazon's recommendation engine are an excellent way to discover things to read, while social media, at its best, is like having thousands of unpaid assistants scouring the globe for content you're likely to find particularly fascinating. But the result, as I assume you'd agree if you've been active online these last few decades, hasn't been greater sanity or calm. Since the incoming supply of genuinely interesting stuff is effectively limitless, improving the efficiency with which you discover it just means you're bombarded with books, articles, podcasts and videos that seem like they might contain a nugget of wisdom critical for your happiness or professional success. The challenge isn't to locate a few needles of relevance in a haystack of dross. The challenge, in the words of the technology critic Nicholas Carr, is figuring out how to deal, day in day out, with 'haystack-sized piles of needles.'

It's tempting to wonder if the solution might lie in consuming things more quickly, perhaps by listening to audiobooks on double-speed, or by pursuing the dream, which is largely all it is, of learning to speed-read. (Recall Woody Allen's line about taking a speed-reading course, then tackling *War and Peace*: 'It's about Russia.') But there's far too much content for that. 'You could cut out every single possible nanosecond of silence and never make it through,' observes one audio specialist, in a tirade against the 'trim silence' feature on certain podcast apps, which permits listeners to eliminate any slivers of reflective silence that might have made it into an episode. 'You will never be efficient enough to [hear] it all before you're gone.' Moving more quickly through an infinite incoming supply of something never gets you to the end of it. Because you're processing more of it, faster, and without ever achieving the satisfaction of reducing it, you're just left feeling more scattered and stressed.

Fortunately, there are three pieces of advice for navigating a world of infinite information that are more genuinely helpful. The first is to *treat your to-read pile like a river, not a bucket*. That is to say: think of your backlog not as a container that gradually fills up, and that it's your job to empty, but as a stream that flows past you, from which you get to pick a few choice items, here and there, without feeling guilty for letting all the others float by. In any case, when you stop to think about it, there's something slightly arbitrary about *which* repositories of information we define as guilt-inducing buckets in the first place. I know several older people who appear to believe that if a physical newspaper or magazine makes its way into their home, they have a moral duty to read it. I've felt similarly tormented by long lists of web-browser bookmarks. Yet none of us seems remotely bothered that we'll never make it through the 25 million books currently held by the Library of Congress. (They're housed, along with other printed matter, on more than 800 miles of shelves.) Clearly, the mere existence of something readable creates no obligation to read it – and nor does the fact that it's entered your awareness, your web browser, or your home.

The second piece of advice is to *resist the urge to stockpile knowledge*. At least where non-fiction sources are concerned, it's easy to fall into the assumption that the point of reading or listening to things is to add to your storehouse of knowledge and insights, like a squirrel hoarding nuts, in preparation for a future when you'll finally get to take advantage of it all. (This attitude prompts some people to develop complicated systems for taking notes on everything they read, which turns reading into a chore, which then perversely leads to their not reading books they'd otherwise enjoy or benefit from, because they can't face taking the notes.) Most of the long-term benefits of reading arise not from facts you insert into your brain, but from the ways in which reading changes you, by shaping your sensibility, from which good work and good ideas will later flow. 'Every book makes a mark,' says the art consultant Katarina Janoskova, 'even if it doesn't stay in your conscious memory.'

The closely related final rule is to remember that *consuming information is a present-moment activity, like everything else*. It's not merely that a fixation on retaining facts is a poor way to reap the benefits of reading. It's also that *any* focus on 'reaping the benefits' risks obscuring the truth that a meaningful life, in the end, has to involve at least some activities we love doing for themselves, here and now. So you needn't always choose to read what's most edifying, or professionally useful, or most enthusiastically endorsed by the arbiters of culture. Sometimes it's OK just to read whatever seems most fun. Spending half an hour reading something interesting, moving, awe-inspiring or merely amusing might be worth doing, not just to improve who you become in the future – though it might do that too – but for the sake of that very half hour of being alive.

You can't care about everything

On staying sane when the world's a mess

> 'The art of being wise is the art of knowing what to overlook.'
>
> — WILLIAM JAMES

In his memoirs, the late French philosopher Raymond Aron recounts a story in which he's strolling through Paris with his wife Suzanne and their newborn daughter, one glorious morning in the 1930s. It's easy to picture the scene – the whole city soaking up the sun, making conversation in the shade of trees, or drinking coffee and smoking at pavement bistro tables. Well, almost the whole city: in the

Jardin du Luxembourg, Aron spots his friend and fellow graduate of the École Normale Supérieure, Simone Weil, seemingly convulsed with grief. The Arons ask what's wrong. 'There is a strike in Shanghai,' Weil responds, eyes brimming with tears, 'and troops fired on the workers!'

Weil, as the scholar Alain Supiot explains, 'was one of those people who never manage to abstract themselves from the torrent of suffering in which humanity finds itself engulfed.' It's not for me to say that Weil was *wrong* to feel such distress about a horror unfolding thousands of miles away, to which she had no personal connection. Some level of concern for the suffering of distant others is plainly laudable, and to many of her admirers today, the Jewish-Catholic-Marxist mystic is regarded as a saint. But I'm on safer ground asserting that most of us, including me, would be entirely unable to function were we to experience the emotional impact of every killing or act of injustice around the world as if it had befallen a loved one. And yet that isn't too far from what's increasingly demanded of us today.

Maybe this seems like a strange claim to make about an era that's more often characterized as unprecedentedly self-centered and heartless. Thanks to digital technology, though, it's also a time in which, assuming you're the kind of person who considers it your duty to care about *anything* beyond the walls of your home, you're liable to be asked to care, with maximum intensity, about *everything*.

Partly, that's simply because we're more connected than ever, so that anyone scrolling a social media platform can be instantaneously invited to care about more human suffering than the greatest saints in history would have encountered over the course of their whole lives. But it's also specifically a consequence of the online 'attention economy,' in which the truly valuable commodity – the thing from which advertisers and social media firms and many news organizations stand to make their money – isn't the news itself, but your attention. By now, we understand that this arrangement boosts the prominence of pointless celebrity feuds, polarizing conspiracy theories, and videos of people humiliating themselves in public: it hardly matters whether or not a story is important, so long as it's compelling. What's less obvious is how the same dynamic puts pressure on even the most honorable media organizations and activist groups to exaggerate the importance of every story or cause, because each of them is effectively locked with every other in an arms race for your attention. The result is that even when some event in the news is legitimately extremely serious, you can be sure it'll be presented as even worse than that – except in those corners of the internet where there are more clicks to be gained by just as misleadingly denying its existence altogether.

It was in 2016, after the election of Donald Trump and the Brexit referendum result, that I first began to notice a bizarre effect of all this in myself, and more acutely in certain friends and acquaintances. It wasn't simply that people were addicted to doomscrolling (although they certainly were). It was that they'd started 'living inside the news.' The news had become the psychological center of gravity in their lives – more real, somehow, than the world of their home, friends, and careers, to which they dropped in only sporadically before returning to the main event. They seemed significantly more personally involved in whether Trump would fire his

Secretary of State, or who he might nominate for the Supreme Court, than in any of the local or personal dramas unfolding in their workplaces or families or neighborhoods. Their motives were generally good, so it seems a little churlish to point out that this behavior in no way makes the world a better place. Living inside the news *feels* like doing your duty and being a good citizen. But you can stay informed on ten minutes a day; scrolling any more than that risks becoming disempowering and paralyzing, and certainly eats up time you could have spent making a difference. The Canadian writer David Cain envisions a different way of doing things:

> Imagine if all the available 'public concern' for a given issue could be collected in a huge rain barrel ... and redistributed among fewer people. Instead of having 50 million people care seriously about an issue for all of six hours, you could distill that 300 million hours of public concern into, say, 3,000 people who made it a primary moral concern for a decade ... We can't reallocate public concern like rain-barrel water [but] maybe each of us, within ourselves, can become a little more focused. Imagine if it was normal for each person to focus ten times as deeply on one or two issues at a time, rather than taking on the emotional burden of dozens ... [and] feeling helpless about 'the state of the world.'

In other words, pick your battles, and don't feel bad about doing so. By embracing your limitations in this way, you'll be in a position to do more to fight the battles you do pick, and also thereby to feel better about yourself, than the person who tries to care about everything. (Who may be largely focused, in any case, on trying to *show* that he or she cares about everything.) My favorite example here concerns a former sneaker-firm executive and dedicated Trump opponent named Erik Hagerman, profiled in the *New York Times* in 2018, where he was presented as a kind of anti-Simone Weil: instead of trying to absorb the whole world's pain, he'd opted to live as if the upheavals in American public life weren't happening at all. He consumed no news whatsoever, and when he left his home in rural Ohio to get coffee and a scone from his local café, he wore headphones playing white noise, so he couldn't hear fellow customers talking politics. Unsurprisingly, conservative news outlets condemned him as a whining liberal, while progressive ones labelled him a monster of privilege. One journalist disparaged Hagerman as 'the most selfish person in America,' and further fumed: 'Not everyone gets to be ignorant. People whose families are being torn apart by [US immigration policy] don't get to be ignorant. People who are affected by gun violence don't get to be ignorant.'

And yet might Hagerman simply have accurately assessed his capacity for care, and then decided to apportion it more effectively than most of us do? In his downtime, the *Times* explained, he was busy restoring an area of wetlands he'd purchased; when he was finished, he planned to preserve it for public access. He predicted the project would require most of his savings. There are more selfish ways to spend a life.

It used to be said about certain horrifying news events

that 'if you're not outraged, you're not paying attention.' But that's a relic of a time when people had attention to spare, and when it wasn't in the vested interests of media outlets to stoke as much outrage as possible. In an age of attention scarcity, the greatest act of good citizenship may be learning to withdraw your attention from everything except the battles you've chosen to fight.

Let the future be the future

On crossing bridges when you come to them

'What is anxiety? It is the next day. With whom, then, does the pagan contend in anxiety? With himself, with a delusion, because the next day is a powerless nothing if you yourself do not give it your strength.'

— SØREN KIERKEGAARD

I can remember exactly where I was when I was struck by the full force of a phrase I must have heard, by that point, a thousand times since childhood: 'We'll cross that bridge when we come to it.' I was waiting for a train at the Union Street subway station in Brooklyn, and fretting in my customary manner, this time about the logistics of a forthcoming move between apartments, although it could have been anything. I was waiting to hear if I'd be able to move on the date I wanted, which I couldn't know until the departing tenant had finalized her plans. Suddenly, all this mental fidgeting struck me as absurd, and in a profound way: I was seeking to reassure myself on a question about which, as philosophers like to say, there was no 'fact of the matter.' It wasn't merely that I didn't know the answer yet; it was that no answer would even exist until a point in the near future. This was a bridge I had no option but to cross when I came to it.

Certain forms of human finitude are easy enough to perceive: our limited amount of time, for example, or our limited ability to control how others act. But it can be harder to notice one of the most significant ones – the way we're hopelessly trapped in the present, confined to *this* temporal locality, unable even to stand on tiptoes and peer over the fence into the future, to check that everything's all right there. This is deeply disturbing, because it means that we suffer from what the psychologist Robert Saltzman calls 'total vulnerability to events.' It's always the case that absolutely anything, or at least anything consistent with the laws of physics, could happen at any moment. In the very next second, 'a beloved friend or companion could be lost forever in an instant,' writes Saltzman, rubbing salt into the wound. It may not be remotely likely that, say, a sinkhole will yawn open and swallow me on my next trip to purchase groceries; but the unavoidable truth is that I can never rule it out. My wife vividly recalls the moment in her teens, after a childhood steeped in moviegoing, when she realized that if something obliteratingly awful were to happen to her, or to someone she loved, it wouldn't be foreshadowed by sinister film music. No: it would just happen. Anything always could.

The main way we try to resist this horrifying state of affairs is by worrying. What is worry, at its core, but the activity of a mind attempting to picture every single bridge that might possibly have to be crossed in future, then trying to figure out how to cross it? The compulsive and repetitious character of worry arises from the fact that for finite humans, this goal is doubly impossible. Firstly, we can't possibly think of every challenge we might end up facing. Secondly, even if we could, the solace we crave could only come from knowing we'd made it safely over the bridges in question – which we can't ever know until we've actually crossed them. Thus, as Hannah Arendt writes, 'constantly bound by craving and fear to a future full of uncertainties, we strip each present moment of its calm, its intrinsic import, which we are unable to enjoy. And so, the future destroys the present.'

There's a tendency, in self-help circles, to portray worry as an act of irrational foolishness; but in the prehistoric environment in which humans evolved, it made perfect sense. Things happened fast there. If you heard a rustling in the bushes, it was vital to fixate on wondering what might be causing it, a reaction that was accompanied by a spike of anxiety: that response would have kept you alert until a few seconds later, when you could confirm it was only a harmless bird. The trouble is that today we live in what's been called a 'delayed-return environment,' in which it can take weeks or months to discover if a potential problem is real or not. If your worry concerns something less immediate than a rustling in the bushes – if it's about, say, whether your application for funding will be approved when the grants committee meets the month after next – then there's no useful behavior for your anxiety to motivate, and nowhere for it to go. So it lingers and loops, distracting you from the tasks that might actually have helped you construct a more secure future.

Just because certainty about the future is off the table, though, it doesn't mean you can't feel confident in your abilities to deal with the future when it does eventually arrive. As the celebrated Stoic emperor Marcus Aurelius reassures readers of his *Meditations*: 'Never let the future disturb you. You will meet it, if you have to, with the same weapons of reason which today arm you against the present.' You could say the worrier gets things exactly backwards. He's so terrified that he might not be able to rely on his inner resources, later on, when he reaches a bridge that needs crossing, that he makes superhuman efforts to bring the future under his control right now. In fact he should devote less energy to manipulating the future, and have more faith in his capacity to handle things once the challenge actually arrives. *If* it arrives, that is. Marcus's phrase 'if you have to' is a useful reminder that most of the bridges we worry about never end up needing to be crossed at all.

The fact that you can't cross bridges before you come to them is liable to seem dispiriting, as if it leaves us with no option but to keep trudging vulnerably into the fog, trying not to think about sinkholes. But it contains a hidden gift. After all, if you're hopelessly trapped in the present, it follows that your responsibility can only ever be to the very next moment – that your job is always simply to do what Carl Jung calls 'the next and most necessary thing' as best you can.

Now and then, to be sure, the next most necessary thing might be a little judicious planning for the future. But you can do that, then let go of it, and move on; you needn't try to live mentally ten steps ahead of yourself, straining to feel sure about what's coming later. You get to stop fretting about literally everything other than how to spend the next instant in a wise, enjoyable or otherwise meaningful fashion. Finite human beings need never worry about anything else.

Week Two

Taking Action

'Action isn't a burden to be hoisted up and lugged around on our shoulders. It is something we are. The work we have to do can be seen as a kind of coming alive.'

— JOANNA MACY

DAY EIGHT

Decision-hunting

On choosing a path through the woods

'Concerning one's dharma, one should not vacillate!'

— THE BHAGAVAD GITA

I n case it's not clear by now, I'll emphasize it again: embracing your limitations isn't a matter of settling for less in life. It's not about passively sitting back and letting things happen to you. I refuse to endorse the claim – variously attributed to Kurt Vonnegut, the Dalai Lama and Pastor Rick Warren, and popular among self-styled spiritual types – that 'we are human beings, not human doings.' The whole point of facing the truth about finitude is that it gets easier to spend more of your time on worthwhile and life-enriching activities once you're no longer trying to do all of them, or do them perfectly, or do them with the secret agenda of achieving a feeling of security or control. That's why our focus, this week, is on the art of taking imperfect action. And I know of no better way to start doing that – especially when you're mired in procrastination, or unable to figure out your next move – than to go looking for some kind of decision you could make. And then make it.

There is a vast academic and popular literature on the art of decision-making, but much of it misses the point by treating decisions as things that just sort of *come along*. It's as though you're sitting behind your enormous desk in the executive suite, sipping your coffee, and every so often an underling hurries into the office, clutching a manila folder containing a decision you must make. Perhaps this is how presidents and captains of industry experience decisions – and even for the rest of us, it's true that decisions do occasionally land on our desk, figuratively speaking, in this manner. Should you accept the job offer? Say yes to the proposal of marriage? Hand over your wallet to the mugger, or decline? Far more frequently, though, the life-enhancing route is to think of decisions not as things that come along, but as things to go hunting for. In other words: to operate on the assumption that somewhere, in the confusing morass of your work or your life, lurks at least one decision you could make, right now, in order to get unstuck and get moving.

The executive coach Steve Chandler, in his book *Time Warrior*, refers to this sort of decision-making as 'choosing,' which he contrasts with the similar-sounding but actually very different activities of 'trying to decide,' or figuring out what to do. You could fritter months trying to work out how best to begin the screenplay you've been meaning to write, and you might never succeed. But to take the three opening scenes you've been pondering and just choose one is the work of a moment, and unequivocally within your capabilities. Or suppose you've been trying to decide, vaguely, about whether to leave your job. That's the sort of dilemma over which people spin their wheels for years. But right now, over the course of the next three minutes, it would be easy to choose the person in your social circle who's most likely to have some good advice on the matter, then email them to invite them for coffee. 'Most people believe a deficit in *knowing* is their problem,' Chandler writes. They 'believe that they don't *know* what to do, so it will take time before they do it.' But choosing? 'Takes no time. When you choose you've already chosen.'

Looking at things this way, indeed, you might argue that making a decision is the defining act of the limit-embracing life. As we've already seen, the fact that your time is limited – plus the reality that you can only ever be in one place at any instant – means that in every moment, you're opting not to take a thousand alternative paths through life. From each of these paths branch another thousand alternatives, and so endlessly on, like a vast river delta through which you could follow any one of an immense variety of streams. But only one. That's why indecision can feel so oddly comfortable: it's a form of postponement, a temporary avoidance of the painful sacrifices involved. (Put differently, it's a way of trying to dodge the inevitability of consequences, which we explored on Day Three.) To make a decision – any decision – is to take ownership of the situation instead. It's acknowledging your presence in the kayak, instead of fantasizing about super-yachts. It takes a little willpower, but the reward is usually an immediate boost of motivation, as you withdraw your psychological energies from denial or avoidance and focus them on action. Momentum starts to gather, and each decision proves easier to take than the last.

There are two rules of decision-hunting worth bearing in mind here. The first is that a decision doesn't get to count as a decision until you've done something about it in reality, so as to put some of your discarded alternatives beyond reach. Merely telling yourself you've decided, inside your mind, isn't enough. You have to actually begin drafting the opening scene of the screenplay, setting off down that creative path as opposed to any of the others. You have to actually email your friend about the coffee, thereby transforming your purely private doubt about your job into something that now exists in the external world.

The other rule, however, balancing the first, is that as long as a decision meets that litmus test, it can be as tiny a decision as you like. Grand gestures aren't required. There's no need to leap directly from thinking about a career change to marching into your manager's office to quit. Baby steps are fine; they just have to be real ones. (What the novelist E. L. Doctorow said about novel-writing applies to everything else, too: it's 'like driving a car at night. You never see further than your headlights, but you can make the whole trip that way.') Keep making tiny-but-real decisions, and when it's time to quit, your visit to the boss will be just one more incremental next step.

The topic of deciding and choosing naturally calls to

mind one of the most famous poems ever written, Robert Frost's 'The Road Not Taken.' You know the one: about the two paths diverging in a 'yellow wood,' and how the speaker chooses 'the one less traveled by,' a choice that he says 'made all the difference.' On the standard interpretation, Frost's poem is little more than a clichéd celebration of the American dream. Spurn convention! Do your own thing, believe in yourself, and success is guaranteed! But as the poet David Orr explains, in his book also entitled *The Road Not Taken*, it's really something much stranger. Frost's poem undermines the conventional reading on almost every line. No sooner has the speaker told us about the road less traveled than he admits that, in fact, previous travelers had left the two paths worn 'really about the same.' And on closer examination, he never asserts that his choice of path 'made all the difference' in his life, either. How could he know, since he never got to compare it to the other one? What the speaker of the poem may be saying is that 'ages and ages hence,' when he's an old man, he expects that's what he'll *claim*. Because he'll want to rationalize the choices he made – like everyone always does.

The true insight of Frost's poem, on this interpretation, isn't that you should opt for an unconventional life. It's that the only way to live authentically is to acknowledge that you're inevitably always making decision after decision, decisions that will shape your life in lasting ways, even though you can't ever know in advance what the best choice might be. In fact, you'll never know in hindsight, either – because no matter how great or appalling the consequences of heading down any given path, you'll never learn whether heading down a different one might have brought something better or worse. Even so, to move forward, you still have to choose, and keep on choosing. If the speaker in 'The Road Not Taken' hadn't consciously made some choice, he'd have made a different, unconscious one instead – to remain standing at that fork in the path, frozen in ambivalence, waiting for something to happen.

Finish things

On the magic of completion

'When my husband does the dishes he always leaves some platter in the sink, some surface unwiped. I tried to correct the behavior until I remembered that if I finish everything in my *Work in Progress* folder I'm afraid I'll die.'

— SARAH MANGUSO

There is a mysterious energy in finishing things. Contemplating the matter in advance, you'd assume that seeing a project through to the end might leave you feeling depleted, especially if it's one that's been hanging around for a while. Yet the truth is that completion replenishes energy, rather than using it up. So getting into the habit of finishing what you start creates fuel for further meaningful productivity.

Perfectionists love to begin new endeavors, because the moment of starting belongs to the world of limitlessness: for as long as you haven't done any work on a project, it's still possible to believe that the end result might match the ideal in your mind. You can luxuriate in the feeling of pure potential; it's like opening the curtains, one weekend morning in childhood, to find the streets and gardens blanketed in virgin snow. By contrast, finishing things means slogging your way through the messy, imperfect reality of what the project actually became; the childhood analogy this evokes, for me, is grinding to the end of a history homework essay. (And not because I didn't like history essays: I was a huge nerd, and probably enjoyed them more than playing in the snow. But only *starting* them. Finishing them, mired in disgust at what I'd produced, felt like torture.)

Social psychologists describe what's going on here using the language of 'construal level theory,' which refers to the way we conceive of objects and events as if from different mental altitudes. The classic example concerns summer vacations. Consider how you'd like to spend yours next year, and you're likely to picture it, figuratively speaking, from 30,000 feet: you might see yourself 'going to the beach,' or 'hiking in the mountains,' or 'relaxing as a family.' But when the vacation draws closer, you'll descend a few thousand feet and start focusing in on details: which beach, which mountain trails, which restaurants to eat at, and so forth. Similarly, at the start of any major undertaking, we see it in outline, smooth if a little blurry; it's only as we dig in that we begin to encounter the flaws, the compromises, and the grunt-work involved. At which point we make the error of assuming that a *new* endeavor might be free of such imperfections. Really, of course, what makes the new endeavor more appealing is just that we're seeing it at a mental distance; we fail to realize, in the words of the psychology writer Jude King, that 'every worthwhile goal is supposed to feel hard, unglamorous, unsexy,' at least for some of the time you're actually putting in the work.

And yet, in reality, repeatedly starting but rarely finishing things, or finishing them only under duress, is a recipe for misery. You get fewer worthwhile things done, not least because, whenever you hit a difficult patch in whatever you're doing, there are several other projects to which you can scurry off instead. You never accumulate a track record of accomplishments in which to take pride; and you never benefit from the feedback you'd have received had you shared your work with others. You become filled with self-loathing, and overwhelmed by the number of unfinished items on your plate. People think finishing things 'would drain even more of their energy and they get tired just thinking about it,' Steve Chandler writes. They don't see 'that leaving things unfinished is what's causing the low levels of energy.' (He suggests spending one day robotically completing as much unfinished business as you can: 'Notice at the end of that day how much energy you've got. You'll be amazed.')

The trick to finishing things when the prospect seems overwhelming is simply to redefine what counts as finished. Instead of viewing the completion of a project as something that happens only occasionally, after days or weeks of work, think of your days as consisting in the sequential completion of a series of small 'deliverables.' 'Deliverables' is monstrous business-speak, of course, evoking the soulless milieu in which people talk of cloudifying business-critical learnings and future-proofing core competencies. But that's exactly why I like it. It's so drab that it drains the drama from the act of finishing, recasting it as something so utterly routine you might do it over the course of every day.

To define your next deliverable, clarify some outcome you could attain in a single sitting – in the next few minutes, say, or over an hour or two at most. Then work until you reach it. If you need to send a difficult email, write the email and send it, rather than beginning it then letting it fester in your drafts. For bigger projects, break off a piece: finish the research for the first section of the report; finalize the paint colors for the living room; select a workout plan and schedule your first session at the gym. Do it and be done with it. Put it on your done list, if you like. Then move on.

As you get into the swing of this, completion ceases to be a matter of occasional, stress-filled crescendos of effort, and your days instead involve a low-key process of moving small, clearly defined packages of work across your desk and out the door. Each ending provides an energy-boost for the next. It works so well, I suspect, because it means acting in harmony with reality: for finite humans, every moment is an endpoint of sorts, experienced once then done with forever. Treating what you do with your time as a sequence of tiny comple-tions means falling into line with how things really are. 'Work is done, then forgotten,' says the *Tao Te Ching*. 'There-fore it lasts forever.' You're no longer fighting the current, but letting it carry you forward. Life is less effort that way.

DAY TEN

Look for the life task

On what reality wants

'Going was dying, and staying was dying. When we get
to junctures like that, we had better choose the dying
that enlarges rather than the one that keeps us stuck.'

— JAMES HOLLIS

There's a scene early in Carl Jung's autobiography *Memories, Dreams, Reflections* in which the future pioneer of psychotherapy is crouching behind a bush in the shrubbery of the family home in Switzerland, eavesdropping on his father's conversation with a friend. At this point, the adolescent Jung had been off school for almost six months, owing to mysterious fainting spells somehow connected to his intense fear of mathematics classes. For months, he'd reveled in the time off. 'I was free,' he recalled, 'could dream for hours, be anywhere I liked, in the woods or by the water, or draw.' Just recently, though, he'd had the creeping sense that by staying home he was somehow avoiding life. 'I had the obscure feeling that I was fleeing from myself,' he writes. Then he heard the friend ask his father: 'And how is your son?'

> 'Ah, that's a sad business,' my father said. 'The doctors no longer know what is wrong with him. They think it may be epilepsy. It would be dreadful if he were incurable. I have lost what little I had, and what will become of the boy if he cannot earn his own living?'

Jung recalls being 'thunderstruck' on hearing these words, and knowing immediately what he had to do. 'This was the collision with reality. "Why, then, I must get to work!" I thought suddenly. From that moment on, I became a serious child. I crept away, went to my father's study, took out my Latin grammar, and began to cram with intense concentration.' The fainting fits returned but he plowed on anyway, and eventually they ceased. As the Jungian analyst Deborah Stewart explains, Jung had recognized that resuming his studies was the 'essential life task' that faced him. His character was being tested – and he understood that if he was going to move forward into his life, instead of avoiding it, it was time to get down to work.

The question can be a startlingly powerful one, particularly when you find yourself torn between options, or between external pressures and your own ambitions, or unable, for any other reason, to figure out what to do next: What's the life task here? Never mind what *you* want. What does life want?

(And if the very idea that 'life' might be able to 'want' things strikes you as unforgivably unscientific, then your life task, for the next few paragraphs, is to put your skepticism briefly to one side.)

It would be easy to misinterpret the shrubbery tale as Jung succumbing to parental pressure, or finally submitting to the societal message that hard work is always a virtue (a message that was as popular as you might imagine in his nineteenth-century Swiss Protestant milieu). But that's not what Jungians mean by a life task. By definition, a life task is something *your* life is asking of you; so while it might coincide with your parents' expectations, or your society's ideals, it also very easily might not. As it happens, Jung's moment of insight propelled him in the direction his father also wished him to go. Yet stepping up to a life task might just as easily mean resisting expectations instead. Sometimes what's called for isn't buckling down to your studies, but dropping out of college.

How can you identify your current life task? That must always be a matter of intuition. But there are two signposts that may help. The first is that a life task will be something you can do 'only by effort and with difficulty,' as Jung puts it – and specifically with that feeling of 'good difficulty' that comes from pushing back against your long-established preference for comfort and security. In the words of another Jungian, James Hollis, it may be the kind of endeavor that 'enlarges' you, rather than making you feel immediately happy. This is where you'll need to be honest with yourself. For some people, honoring a life task might mean mustering the boldness to leave a relationship, or a job.

But perhaps you're someone for whom running away from difficult situations is your default behavior; in that case, your task might entail mustering the boldness to stay. Likewise, it *might* mean walking away from your life to become a humanitarian aid worker; but the equally uncomfortable possibility is that the voice telling you to become an aid worker is the internalized voice of societal morality, the one that thinks it knows better than you the sort of contribution you should make. Perhaps your real contribution will be designing jewelry, or writing songs.

The second signpost is that a true life task, though it might be difficult, will be something you can do. If you only have a hundred dollars in the bank, your life task won't require the immediate purchase of thousands of dollars' worth of moviemaking equipment (although it might involve doing something to raise the cash). If you're the single parent of three small children, it won't involve working eighteen-hour days for a tech start-up; and by the same token, if you're unable to have children, it won't involve becoming a biological parent. This helps distinguish the idea of a life task from certain popular notions of 'destiny' or 'calling,' which can leave people feeling as though there's something they're meant to be doing with their lives, but that their life circumstances make it impossible. That can't be the case with a life task, which emerges, by definition, from whatever your life circumstances are. It's what's being asked of *you*, with your particular skills, resources and personality traits, in the place where you actually find yourself.

As for the question of whether this isn't all just woolly, unscientific therapy-talk, the answer is that I don't think it matters. To enquire what your life task might be, at any particular instant, is to switch your perspective in a manner that makes it possible to think new thoughts. It permits you to dig beneath the crust of assumptions that all too easily end up governing a life: that you have no option but to continue on your current career path; or that you mustn't make choices on which others might frown; or that you're obliged to do something extraordinary with your life.

The most remarkable part is that while you might have assumed that complying with a life task would feel oppressive – you're 'complying' with a 'task,' after all – it never does. It gives you the feeling of getting a handle on life, because the life to which you're addressing the question is the one you actually have. It is never the case that there's no next step to take. On some level, I think we always already know when we're hiding out in some domain of life, flinching from a challenge reality has placed before us. The purpose of a question like 'What's the life task here?' is just to haul that knowledge up into the daylight of consciousness, where we can finally do something about it.

DAY ELEVEN

Just go to the shed
On befriending what you fear

'We cannot change anything unless we accept it.'

— C. G. JUNG

I t can be alarming to realize just how much of life gets shaped by what we're actively trying to avoid. We talk about 'not getting around to things' as if it were merely a failure of organization, or of will. But often the truth is that we invest plenty of energy in making sure we never get around to them. It's an old story: some task, or some entire domain of life, makes you anxious whenever you think about it, so you just don't go there. You're worried you might have less money in the bank than you'd assumed, so you refrain from checking your balance at all. Or you're scared that a pain in your abdomen might be the sign of something serious, so you avoid seeing a doctor. Or you're worried that raising a sensitive subject with your partner could lead to a blazing row – so you never do. Several times, I've caught myself avoiding checking my email, for fear of discovering a message from someone impatient I haven't replied to yet.

Rationally speaking, this kind of avoidance makes no sense at all. If you really do have an alarmingly low bank balance, or the pain really is something serious, confronting the situation is the only way you can begin to do something about it; and there's no better strategy than avoiding your inbox to ensure that someone will, eventually, lose patience with your failure to reply. The more you organize your life around not addressing the things that make you anxious, the more likely they are to develop into serious problems – and even if they don't, the longer you fail to confront them, the more unhappy time you spend being scared of what might be lurking in the places you don't want to go. It's ironic that this is known, in self-help circles, as 'remaining in your comfort zone,' because there's nothing comfortable about it. In fact, it entails accepting a constant background tug of *dis*comfort – an undertow of worry that can sometimes feel useful or virtuous, though it isn't – as the price you pay to avoid a more acute spike of anxiety.

What you should do in such situations, I've learned, is just go to the shed.

I learned this way of thinking about avoidance from Paul Loomans, a Dutch Zen monk who explains it in a lovely book entitled *Time Surfing*. Loomans refers metaphorically to the tasks or areas of life you're avoiding as 'gnawing rats.' But he rejects the conventional advice about dealing with them, which is to man/woman up and confront your rats – to get over yourself, in other words, and to attack the problem with brute force. The trouble is that this simply replaces one kind of adversarial relationship with your gnawing rats ('Stay away from me!') with another ('I'm going to destroy you!'). And that's a recipe for more avoidance over the long term, because who wants to spend their life fighting rats? Loomans's surprising advice is to befriend them instead. Turn towards your gnawing rats. Forge a relationship with them.

But how, exactly, do you forge a relationship with a metaphorical gnawing rat? It might mean finding the least intimidating way to get stuck into it, or asking someone else for help. But it might equally entail something as seemingly passive and ineffective as merely closing your eyes and visualizing yourself taking an action. All you're seeking is some way to 'go there,' psychologically speaking: to begin to accept, on an emotional level, that the situation in question is already a part of your reality, no matter how fervently you might wish that it weren't. Loomans gives the example of a person whose long-neglected shed, filled with junk, is becoming a source of mounting anxiety and guilt:

> The advice here is: go into the shed. Don't do anything yet, just look around. Observe and take stock. Make the space your own. And [...] the first solutions will present themselves. A number of items will change hands and be donated to others. Other things will wait until that Saturday afternoon when you say to yourself, 'And now it's time to clean

out the shed.' You don't dread it any more, but are actually looking forward to it.

It's worth noting, I think, that 'befriending your rats' isn't just another way of expressing the timeworn advice to break an intimidating task down into smaller, more manageable chunks. When you do that, you're reducing the anxiety you feel by reducing the scale of the threat; it's like separating one rat off from the rest of the pack, in order to more effectively stab it to death. By contrast, to befriend a rat is to defuse the anxiety you feel by transforming the kind of relationship you have with it. You turn it into an unobjectionable part of your reality. Whereupon a gnawing rat, in Loomans's terminology, becomes a 'white sheep' – a harmless, docile, fluffy creature that follows you around until you decide to do something about it. Everyone has an assortment of not-yet-begun or not-yet-completed projects that would benefit from their attention, because that's the nature of being a finite human. But there's no need for them to torment you. Once you've established a relationship with them, they become white sheep, and can just patiently wait their turn.

One excellent practical way to befriend a gnawing rat is to ask yourself what you'd truly be *willing* to do, to address some fear-inducing challenge in your life. In the early 1970s, the cognitive psychologist Virginia Valian found herself so paralyzed by work anxiety that she couldn't write a word of her PhD thesis – until she stopped trying to make herself work in the way she thought she was meant to, and asked herself instead how much time she was prepared to spend on it each day:

> I talked about it with J, the man I live with, and he suggested three hours. Three hours! The very thought gave me an anxiety attack. How about two hours? Two hours! The very thought . . . One hour? More reasonable, but still not possible. Half an hour? Getting closer but still too much. Fifteen minutes? Fifteen minutes. Fifteen minutes. Now there was a figure I could imagine. A nice solid amount of time, an amount of time I knew I could live through every day.

People laughed when Valian told them of her fifteen-minute-a-day plan, because it sounded pathetic. In fact it was the opposite. Asking yourself what it would actually entail to befriend the gnawing rats in your life is an act requiring real courage – more courage, perhaps, than the standard confrontational approach, which feels less like reconciling yourself to reality and more like getting into a bar fight with it. Befriending your rats is a gentle strategy, but there's nothing submissive about it. It's a pragmatic way to maximize your room for maneuver, and your capacity to make progress on the work you care about, by becoming ever more willing to acknowledge that things are as they are, whether you like it or not.

Rules that serve life

On doing things dailyish

'We read that monks should not drink wine at all, but since the monks of our day cannot be convinced of this, let us at least agree to drink moderately, and not to the point of excess ...'

— RULE OF SAINT BENEDICT

I once got the chance to interview Jerry Seinfeld, and so, naturally, I asked him about the 'Seinfeld Strategy,' the amazing productivity secret that supposedly explained his prolific joke-writing and global success. The basic technique is as follows: every day that you manage to dedicate at least some time to your central creative goal – in Seinfeld's case, that meant writing jokes for his stand-up act – you mark a big red X in your calendar. Do it every day, and after a week or two, you'll have a pleasing chain of Xs. From then on, the rule is not to break the chain. I wanted to know how Seinfeld had come up with this idea, which by then had generated hundreds of admiring articles and posts, and several apps designed to implement the system digitally. To be honest, I was also half-hoping he might impart some additional extra detail, a tweak or a refinement to the technique that I could use to supercharge its effectiveness.

It turned out that the 'Seinfeld Strategy' was a throwaway remark he'd made to an aspiring comic at a comedy club one night, decades earlier, then promptly forgotten about completely.

'It's so dumb it doesn't even seem to be worth talking about!' Seinfeld told me. 'If you're a runner and you want to be a better runner, you say, well, I'll run every day, and I'll mark an X on the calendar every day I run! I can't believe this was useful information to anybody. Really? There are people who think "I'll just sit around and do absolutely nothing, and somehow the work will get done"?' In the world of personal productivity advice, the Seinfeld Strategy had come to refer to the idea that you should work on your main project, every single day, without fail. But the actual Seinfeld's position was just the obvious one that if you want to get good at something, you should do it a lot, preferably more days than not.

A much better rule – indeed, one I think more accurately reflects Seinfeld's approach to his work – is to do things *dailyish*. I'm borrowing the word from Dan Harris, host of the meditation podcast *Ten Percent Happier*, who suggests it whenever people ask him how often they ought to be meditating. If you're the ambitious type, 'dailyish' might strike you as a little self-indulgent. It isn't. If anything, it's the Seinfeld

Strategy that's self-indulgent, because at the moment you set it in motion, you flatter yourself that you're going to be able to follow it impeccably, day after day – even though, were you to reflect on it, you'd probably agree that your life is too unpredictable for that, and your moods too much of a roller-coaster. 'Dailyish' is a much more resilient rule: it's less of a high-wire act, where one mistake could end everything. But emotionally speaking, it's an unsettling rule to follow – because doing something dailyish requires sacrificing your fantasies of perfection in favor of the uncomfortable experience of making concrete, imperfect progress, here and now. In any case, 'dailyish' isn't synonymous with 'just do it whenever you feel like it.' Deep down, you know that doing something twice per week doesn't qualify as dailyish, while five times per week does, and in busy periods, three or four times per week might get to count. So you're still putting some pressure on yourself. But, crucially, what you're not doing is expecting the rule to somehow force the action.

And that's the key distinction here, I think: the unstated appeal of a lot of productivity advice, very much including the Seinfeld Strategy, lies in the bewitching idea that there might be a rule, or a set of rules, that would force accomplishment to occur, rendering it inevitable and automatic. We yearn for such a rule, not generally because we're lazy, but because we don't fully trust ourselves to get the right things done without one. Maybe you lack confidence that you know how to do your work, so you hope that rigidly following a rule might serve as a substitute for that missing knowledge. Maybe you're a self-punishing perfectionist, who demands from yourself a flawless track record, so you want a rule to help ensure you never put a foot wrong. Or maybe you don't really want to do your work at all, but you just think that you ought to want to do it, so you're seeking a system to try to force the missing desire into existence. We want a rule to shoulder the burden of living on our behalf. It's a quid pro quo: we'll follow it religiously and, in return, won't have to take so much moment-to-moment responsibility for making the most of our lives.

Yet, on reflection, no such rule could possibly exist; however much we might sometimes long to outsource the task of living, we never can. Think about it: even the most hidebound rule-follower, dutifully implementing an intricate schedule or set of behavioral guidelines, is still choosing to keep on following them in every moment. They could always opt not to. Like it or not, you're always in charge of the kayak.

Saint Benedict of Nursia, whose rulebook for organizing the communal life of a Christian monastery remains the one followed by many Catholic orders to this day, appears to have undergone a midlife realization of just this nature. Benedict sought to create monastic communities as bulwarks against the immorality that appalled him in sixth-century Europe. But early experiences led him to radically alter his approach to the challenge. As a pious younger man, the story goes, he first organized a group of novice monks under a framework of rules so demanding that several of them conspired to try to poison him – twice. By contrast, the Rule of Saint Benedict, the one he wrote in old age and which is still in use, remains relevant because it's a model of moderation, elegantly balancing the need for order with the need for individual freedom, and a monk's need for solitude with the universal human need for a social life. It also recognizes, in the beautifully forbearing passage quoted above, that monks, like many of the rest of us, enjoy a drink from time to time. Sometime in the aftermath of those poisonings, Benedict apparently understood that the point isn't to spend your life serving rules. The point is for the rules to serve life.

'Dailyish' is one that does. In not insisting on your doing something absolutely every day, it shifts the focus away from the ultimately meaningless question of whether or not you have an unbroken chain of red Xs, and back to the life it's supposed to be serving – to the thing you're seeking to bring into existence, whether that's a piece of writing, a work of art, a happy family, a healthier body, or anything else. In any case, does anyone *really* believe that Jerry Seinfeld owes his success to his assiduous observance of a productivity technique he happened to stumble across? Of course not. He owes it to talent, and maybe a modicum of luck, and then to the willingness to keep showing up and developing that talent, more days than not, in the unpredictable context of his real life. Obviously, the goal was never a chain of red Xs. It was making people laugh.

DAY THIRTEEN

Three hours

On finding focus in the chaos

'Every morning, therefore, at about 9.30 after breakfast each of us, as if moved by a law of unquestioned nature, went off and "worked" until lunch at one. It is surprising how much one can produce in a year, whether of buns or books or pots or pictures, if one works hard and professionally for three and a half hours every day for 330 days [a year]. That was why, despite her disabilities, Virginia was able to produce so very much.'

— LEONARD WOOLF

If rules should serve life, rather than the other way around, it follows that you shouldn't expect there to be many one-size-fits-all rules for making the most of your time. Everybody's life is different, after all, and no individual life remains the same for very long. Still, there's one rule that comes close. If you're a 'knowledge worker' – that is, if you spend your days doing things with computers and words and ideas, as opposed to, say, building houses out of bricks – then you'll make the most progress, and cover the most ground, if you limit yourself to about three or four hours of intense mental focus each day.

It's a little unnerving, to be honest, how frequently this specific range of hours crops up in historical accounts of the daily routines of artists, authors, scientists, composers, and others. There's Charles Darwin, at work on the theory of natural selection in his study at Down House outside London, concentrating for two ninety-minute periods and one one-hour period each day; and Virginia Woolf, writing for three and a half hours after a leisurely breakfast, producing nine novels, around fifty short stories, three book-length essays and scores of shorter works, despite ending her own life at fifty-nine. The mathematician Henri Poincaré focused intensely from ten to twelve in the morning, and from five to seven in the evening, then called it a day. Charles Dickens, Thomas Jefferson, Alice Munro and J. G. Ballard all engaged in focused work for a similar stretch of time, as did Anthony Trollope, who claimed, somewhat irritatingly, that he managed to write 250 words every fifteen minutes during the three-hour stint he put in each morning, before heading to his job at the post office. 'Three hours a day,' Trollope observed, 'will produce as much as a man ought to write.' Several of these examples come from Alex Pang's book *Rest*, where he mentions countless others, and assembles research that helps explain why: because intense focus uses up energy;

because it's more effective to focus intensely during only your peak hours, rather than half-heartedly all day; and because creativity appears to depend partly on processes taking place in your brain while you're *not* focusing. (Limiting the time allotted to high-stakes work also helps reduce the feeling of being intimidated or oppressed by it, which causes some people to procrastinate.)

There'd be little point in seeking to emulate the entire daily routine of any of these figures, most of whom had retinues of servants, and/or a wife, to handle life's humdrum business, so they could spend vast portions of their downtime strolling the countryside, playing tennis, or drinking cocktails. But the near-uniformity of their hours of deep focus suggests what I've come to think of as the 'three-to-four-hour rule' for getting creative work done. It has two parts. The first is to try – to whatever degree your situation permits – to ringfence a three- or four-hour period each day, free from appointments or interruptions. The equally important second part is not to worry about imposing much order on the rest of the day: to accept that your other hours will probably be characterized by the usual fragmentary chaos of life.

This straightforward approach encapsulates more limit-embracing wisdom than might at first be apparent. To begin with, it acknowledges the reality that most of us don't have the capacity for more than a few daily hours of intense concentration. But it also respects limitation in another important way: it frees you from the futile perfectionistic struggle to try to make the whole day unfold in accordance with your desires. It respects the fact that your work demands focus; but at the same time, it spares you from having to spend most of your hours in a defensive posture, braced against each new email, phone call, or serendipitous encounter in the hallway.

The most powerful effect of the rule, though, might be the way in which it limits the possibility of hurry. It pushes back against the ubiquitous modern urge to get as much done as possible as fast as possible, in obedience to the inner voice whispering that just maybe, if you really went hell-for-leather for the next few days, you might get on top of the work once and for all. That approach fails, not least because rest and good moods are both essential for sustained and successful work. The words of the economist Adam Smith, here giving advice to the 'masters' of 'workmen,' apply just as much to the question of how hard to drive oneself:

> If masters would always listen to the dictates of reason and humanity, they have frequently occasion rather to moderate, than to animate the application of many of their workmen. It will be found, I believe, in every sort of trade, that the man who works so moderately, as to be able to work constantly, not only preserves his health the longest, but, in the course of the year, executes the greatest quantity of work.

The three-to-four-hour rule functions, too, as a reminder of the profound truth that for finite humans the work is never done. A central point of the Jewish and Christian tradition of the Sabbath is that you have to stop anyway – not because you've finished, but just because it's time to stop. How far you can check out of the culture of overwork will be context-dependent, of course. But regardless of context, you can choose not to psychologically collaborate with that culture. You can abandon the delusion that if you just managed to squeeze in a couple more hours of focused work, you'd finally reach the commanding position of mastering it all. The truly valuable skill is the one the three-to-four-hour rule helps to instill: not the capacity to push yourself harder, but the capacity to stop and recuperate, despite the discomfort of knowing that the work remains unfinished.

This is the spirit embodied by one monk at the Monastery of Christ in the Desert, in New Mexico, interviewed by the writer Jonathan Malesic for his book *The End of Burnout*. The monks' daily work period ends at 12.40 p.m. (and no prizes for guessing when it begins: about three hours earlier). Malesic writes:

> I asked Father Simeon, a monk who spoke with a confidence cultivated through the years he spent as a defense attorney, what you do when the 12.40 bell rings but you feel that your work is undone.
>
> 'You get over it,' he replied.

DAY FOURTEEN

Develop a taste for problems

On never reaching the trouble-free phase

'Beyond the mountains, more mountains.'

– HAITIAN PROVERB

'It's always something!' was the American comedian Gilda Radner's catchphrase, and her avowed stance towards the cancer that eventually killed her. Jewish humor excels at this sardonic acceptance of life's trials, but it's far from a dismissive shrug of resignation: it expresses the deep understanding that grappling with all the some-things is what life is fundamentally about. It truly *is* always something, even if most of the time, thankfully, it's something less frightening than a cancer diagnosis. The trick is learning to appreciate this situation for the cosmic joke, and the daily reality, that it is.

The author and podcast host Sam Harris recalls being at lunch with a friend, moaning on about the various problems he was confronting in his work, when she interrupted him mid-flow. 'Were you really expecting to have no more problems at some point in your life?' she asked. Harris realized, with a start, that he had been subconsciously proceeding on the basis that such a time would eventually arrive. 'I was tacitly assuming that I should be able to get rid of all my problems,' he recalled later. 'Even though this sounds ridiculous, that was implicit to my thinking and my emotional life, to the way I was meeting each new problem.'

He's surely far from alone. I suspect that most of us, except perhaps the very Zen or the very elderly, move through our days with a similar if largely unconscious assumption that at some point – maybe not soon, but eventually – we'll make it to the phase of life which won't involve confronting an endless fusillade of things to deal with. The unfortunate consequence is that we experience our ordinary problems – the bills to pay, the minor conflicts to resolve, each little impediment that stands between us and realizing our goals – as doubly problematic. First, there's the problem itself. But then there's the way in which the very existence of any such problems undermines our yearning to feel perfectly secure and in control. So we spend our lives leaning into the future, unconsciously deeming whatever's happening now to be fundamentally flawed, because it's marred by too many problems. And quite possibly deeming ourselves to be fundamentally flawed, too – or else wouldn't we have figured out some way to eliminate all these problems by now? Yet the reality, as Harris goes on, is that '. . . life is an unending series of complications, so it doesn't make any sense to be surprised by the arrival of the next one.'

You needn't reflect for long on the subject of human limitation to see that the existence of problems simply follows, unavoidably, from the facts of finitude; at the most abstract level, 'problem' is just the word we apply to any situation in which we confront the limits of our capacity to control how things unfold. (We might triumph over any given problem, of course; but if we had total control, we'd never confront them in the first place.) It takes only a little further reflection to see that we wouldn't really want life to be otherwise. It would be nice to be able to skip the scariest or most overwhelming problems. But to face no problems at all would leave you with nothing worth doing; so you might even say that coming up against your limitations, and figuring out how to respond, is precisely what makes a life meaningful and satisfying. There's a clue to be found in the leisure activities to which many of us gravitate, after a workday spent resenting our problems: we play board games, or watch police dramas, or learn musical instruments, or try our hand at cooking new dishes – none of which would be any fun if it weren't for the problem-solving involved.

When I let myself be permeated by the thought that the problem-free time might never be coming, my first reaction is one of peevishness: 'Wait, that's not what I signed up for!' But swiftly thereafter comes an unclenching. If I no longer have to fight against the sheer fact of encountering problems, because that's a battle I'll never win, I get to dive more fully, perhaps even with relish, into the problems I actually have. I no longer have to remain in the posture – absurd for finite humans, for whom time is so precious – of trying to get the present out of the way, en route to the problem-free future. And I am free to aspire not to a life without problems, but to a life of ever more interesting and absorbing ones.

A friend of mine vividly recalls the uplifting and energizing moment when, feeling burdened like Harris by the endless problems that seemed to get in the way of her doing her job, it dawned on her that the problems *were* the job. Anyone, or a piece of software, could do her job, if it weren't for the problems. Her unique contribution lay in her capacity for solving them.

Beyond the mountains, there are always more mountains, at least until you reach the final mountain before your time on earth comes to an end. In the meantime, few things are more exhilarating than mountaineering.

Week Three

Letting Go

'Life completely unhindered by anything
manifests as pure activity.'

— KŌSHŌ UCHIYAMA

DAY FIFTEEN

What if this were easy?

On the false allure of effort

'Not everything that is more difficult is more meritorious.'

— ATTRIBUTED TO SAINT THOMAS AQUINAS

Years ago, while researching a book on the pitfalls of positive thinking, I attended a motivational seminar in a basketball stadium in Texas, entitled, appropriately enough, *Get Motivated!* Needless to say, it was utterly excruciating. (In all honesty, I had strongly suspected it would be; that was why I went.) As pyrotechnics exploded onstage, disco lights flashed, and energetic rock music blasted from the speaker stacks, we were urged to leap from our seats and shout about how motivated we felt. Asking a British person to do such a thing is, of course, a form of torture; and the day didn't improve when the pastor of a megachurch took the podium to instruct us to eliminate the word 'impossible' from our vocabularies. But it was only later that it dawned on me that the problem wasn't solely the simplistic cheesiness of *Get Motivated!* It lay with the whole underlying notion of 'motivation' itself.

In the first week of the journey sketched in this book, we explored the benefits of facing the truth of our finitude, in a world where overwhelm and distraction threaten constantly to derail us; in the second, I sought to share the insights I've found most helpful for taking bold, imperfect action as a finite human. But there's a danger in all such advice: it risks implying that taking meaningful action is necessarily a tough or complex challenge. (If it were straightforward and effortless, why would anyone need advice?) And in one sense, for finite humans, life certainly *is* a tough challenge: you've got severely limited time, and limited control, necessitating hard choices and a tolerance for imperfection and uncertainty. But it's equally true that often the real challenge, in building an accomplished and absorbing life, is learning to let go. Not making things happen, through willpower or effort, but cultivating the willingness to stand out of the way and *let* them happen instead – which is our focus this week.

Consider the basic model of human nature implicit in an event like *Get Motivated!*, and in the idea that worthwhile actions are things you have to 'motivate yourself' in order to do. It's one that assumes you'll need to gin yourself up, to fill yourself with the necessary supply of energy and self-discipline, if you're to avoid sliding back to your default setting of lassitude and time-wasting. (It may also imply that you'll need to regularly replenish that supply – which is hardly a problem, from a business point of view, for the purveyors of motivational seminars, books, and the like.) Meaningful accomplishment, on this account, takes effort. And filling yourself with motivation is one important way to render yourself willing and able to put that effort in.

At first glance, this seems plausible, if somewhat disciplinarian. But in fact, as a way of thinking about your relationship to action, it's a disaster. By defining meaningful tasks as those that always require exertion, and you as the kind of person who needs pushing and prodding to do them, it turns daily life into an ongoing internal battle between the kind of person you'd like to be – energetic, productive – and the kind of person you privately fear yourself to be at the core: prone to backsliding at the first opportunity.

Going through your days in this spirit causes multiple problems, the most obvious being that it makes you much less likely to do satisfying things you'd otherwise have done, and that would have been easy, because you've persuaded yourself they won't be. (Arranging a social gathering, setting up a landing page for your business, booking a trip: in principle, any of these might prove to be the work of moments; that feeling of needing to overcome a looming obstacle of effort might be premised on an illusion.) Moreover, on those occasions when you *do* take action, you do so with more exertion and nervous energy than was really required, because it feels like 'putting in the effort' is inherently virtuous in itself. That's a message we begin receiving early in life: 'My mom used to get really upset at what she perceived as my half-assing,' reads one splendid anonymous comment on a *Washington Post* article by the advice columnist Carolyn Hax. 'I'm 48 now, have a PhD and a thriving and influential career, and I still think there is very very little that's worthy of applying my whole entire ass. I'm not interested in burning myself [out] by whole-assing stuff that will be fine if I half- or quarter-ass it. Being able to achieve maximum economy of ass is an important adult skill.'

The final hazard in the idea that if something matters it must take effort is that it leads, by a seemingly reasonable but entirely bogus reverse logic, to the assumption whatever takes effort must matter. Collapsing on to the sofa at the end of a long day spent deep-cleaning your home, or organizing all your digital files into an orderly hierarchy of folders, it's easy to conclude that you must have used your time well: consider how exhausted you feel! But perhaps your home could have waited another month for a deep clean. And maybe you should never have bothered organizing your files at all, because the search function on your computer is amply good enough to track things down when you need to find them.

And so instead of asking how to summon the energy or motivation or self-discipline to do something that matters to you, it's often more helpful to ask: What if this might be a lot easier than I'd been assuming?

Ironically, this isn't generally an easy question to bring yourself to ask. It feels like cheating; or else it seems obvious to you that the output you'd produce, were you to approach life in this manner, would lack value. So it takes guts: you have to 'be willing to let it be easy,' as Elizabeth Gilbert puts it. Certainly, many tasks and situations are legitimately difficult in themselves, even distressing. The point isn't to deny that reality, but to avoid worsening it – and specifically not to turn the fact that life can be difficult into a judgment of inadequacy on your part. The entrepreneur and podcaster Tim Ferriss phrases the question slightly differently: 'What would this look like if this were easy?' That puts the focus on specifics, on actions you could undertake – and of course the idea isn't to imagine some parallel dimension in which a task might be easy, but to permit yourself to consider the possibility that it might in fact be easy in this one. The New Age author Julia Rogers Hamrick once wrote a book, *Choosing Easy World*, in which she argues it's as simple as repeating a mantra: 'I choose to live in Easy World, where everything is easy.' When some daunting challenge barrels into view, just decide that you're going to experience it as easy instead. I realize that sounds like the worst kind of denial of human limitation, as if you could get your way merely by commanding the universe to fall in line with your desires. In fact, though, it can be surprisingly effective – because it functions not as a mystical command to the universe but as a reminder to yourself not to fall into the old habit of adding complications or feelings of unpleasant exertion where neither need exist.

And we do that all the time. When I fail to take action on things I care about, the reason is sometimes that I lacked the time, or couldn't summon the willpower. But it's at least as likely to be because I spooked myself with visions of the perfect result I thought I needed to achieve, or assumptions about the difficulties involved, thereby blocking action that would otherwise have flowed naturally. For example, I must apparently keep relearning the lesson that when I'm preparing to give a public talk, the best approach is to go for a walk with a notebook, list the points that seem most compelling to me, put them in a sensible order, then practice a few times, enough to get a feel for the talk but not enough to render it stilted or rote. Anything more involved than that is asking for trouble: the end result will be worse. And I vividly recall the moment I realized I'd been overcomplicating my son's fifth birthday party, which had come to feel like a significantly stressful undertaking. What the stress really signaled, I saw, was that I cared about the project, which is entirely different from saying that it needed to be complex or effortful. I like this example because it's actually quite challenging to think of anything *less* difficult than making a success of a five-year-old's birthday party. It's not a tough crowd. If you can get hold of pizza and ice cream, and order some balloons with LEDs in them online, the truly difficult thing would be to screw it up.

The reverse golden rule

On not being your own worst enemy

'Were we to meet this figure socially, this accusatory character, this internal critic, this unrelenting fault-finder, we would think there was something wrong with him. He would just be boring and cruel. We might think that something terrible had happened to him, that he was living in the aftermath, the fallout, of some catastrophe. And we would be right.'

— ADAM PHILLIPS

At this point, we'd better confront the issue that's almost always to blame, deep down, when you find yourself getting in your own way and making things harder than they need to be, which is a lack of self-compassion.

It's time to talk about being kinder to yourself. I know. I *know*. It makes me cringe, too. Unfortunately, that's exactly why the topic mustn't be avoided.

For years, I collected quotations that encapsulated the approach I wanted to take towards the accomplishment of worthwhile things, which was down-to-earth, no-nonsense, unpretentious. One of the best-known examples comes from the artist Chuck Close: 'Inspiration is for amateurs – the rest of us just show up and get to work.' The choreographer George Balanchine liked to say that 'my muse must come to me on union time': he needed to be ready to work when his dancers were there to be choreographed. And there's the line attributed to both William Faulkner and W. Somerset Maugham, which arguably borders on the smug, but that makes a similar point: 'I only write when inspiration strikes. Fortunately it strikes at nine every morning.' *That* was the kind of person I wanted to be: the kind that just got on with things, regardless of how inspired or fired up I happened to feel.

There's definitely some merit in this approach: it helps drain the drama from certain activities, especially those we intimidatingly label 'creative,' making it easier to get over yourself and take action. On the surface, it appears to embody the spirit of imperfectionism. It's just that it never seemed to work particularly well for me, and one day I discovered a blog post, by the meditation teacher Susan Piver, that helped me understand why. Honestly, the title was enough. It was 'Getting stuff done by not being mean to yourself.' Piver was another fan, in theory, of Chuck Close's inspiration-is-for-amateurs philosophy. But she brilliantly evoked its unfortunate flipside, which is that it all too easily morphs into the barked internal command that you ought to be able to do whatever it is you've decided to do, whenever it is you've determined you'll do it, precisely because no inspiration ought to be required – and that if you don't, you're a good-for-nothing worm. 'I've spent a lot of time in my life trying to force myself to do things,' Piver wrote.

> Really good things. Things that are important to me. Things like meditating, journaling, going to the gym, and so on. I set schedules over and over. (I will rise at 5. Meditate, 5.30–6.30. Journal 6.30–7.30. Breakfast 8–9, and so on.) I fail way more than I succeed, which makes me really, really upset. I get angrier and angrier at myself, curse my lack of discipline, shame myself for watching *Battlestar Galactica* (again) instead of writing, delve into my psychology hoping to unearth the seeds of self-sabotage. It spirals out of control until I either give in to lying on the couch or somehow manage to squeeze out a day of discipline according to schedule, whereupon I exhale a half-sigh of relief and immediately begin bullying myself to repeat this tomorrow. IT SUCKS.

And so one day, feeling she had little to lose from trying something different, she asked herself what would happen if she did what she felt like doing, when she felt like doing it – which is another way of asking the question we encountered yesterday: What if this were easy? 'Right away, interestingly, fear swept through me,' she recalls. 'If I'm not vigilant about making myself do stuff, I won't do anything.' But that's not what happened. Following pleasure's lead, she had a *more* productive day, completing the tasks she usually yelled at herself to do, 'only this time, it seemed effortless. I had such a light heart.' Which makes sense, on reflection, because when you do what you feel like doing, you get to use your desires as fuel for action, rather than constantly diverting energy and attention to overcoming them. It's easy to believe that if you let yourself do what you want, you might spend the day scrolling slack-jawed through Instagram. But often the truth is that 'scrolling slack-jawed through Instagram' is what happens after you've told yourself you *can't* do what you want, because you can't afford to or don't deserve to – and you grow so resentful or annoyed by whatever you try to force yourself to do instead that you reach for your phone as a distraction.

Some might object that it's a sign of immense privilege even to be able to contemplate spending the day doing what you feel like doing. And of course this is true, so far as it goes: almost everyone's situation will impose certain limits on their freedom to follow their desires, and it's much worse for some than for others. But it's important to see that this objection itself is often the inner taskmaster in disguise, seeking to make you feel bad for taking advantage of what-ever freedom you do have. There's no prize for failing to spend your time as you wish, to whatever extent you're able, out of a misplaced sense of solidarity with those who cannot.

In any case, treating yourself a little more kindly needn't be anywhere near as self-indulgent as those of us with an allergy to 'self-compassion' tend to assume. It's not about narcissistically declaring yourself to be any more deserving of an easy life than anyone else. It's quite sufficient a challenge to seek to follow what the philosopher Iddo Landau calls the 'reverse golden rule' – that is, not treating yourself in punishing and poisonous ways in which you'd never dream of treating someone else. Can you *imagine* berating a friend in the manner that many of us deem it acceptable to screech internally at ourselves, all day long? Adam Phillips is exactly right: were you to meet such a person at a party, they'd immediately strike you as obviously unbalanced. You might try to get them to leave, and possibly also seek help. It might occur to you that they must be damaged – that in Phillips's words 'something terrible' must have happened to them – for them to think it appropriate to act that way.

Well, something terrible did happen, and the fact that it happens to almost all of us, in one way or another, is no reason to pretend otherwise. From somewhere (your parents, the culture, a religion) you internalized the notion that if you didn't watch yourself like a hawk, disaster might strike. That if you were to cut yourself some slack and follow your own agenda, that might lead to your being abandoned, or humiliated, or overwhelmed by emotions, or financially ruined. The details differ too much from person to person to try to elaborate them here. But wherever the belief comes from, it belongs to the past; it isn't a reasonable assessment of what would be likely to happen now, were you to treat yourself more decently. As Susan Piver discovered, what you generally find, instead, is that you *do* want to honor your commitments, pay your bills, keep yourself physically healthy, and so on – because the person you are, behind all the screeching and yelling, isn't a worthless layabout after all.

Self-indulgent? If anything, it's constantly berating your-self that's the self-indulgent path, reflecting the inner taskmaster's hubristic belief that he or she could bully you into doing anything, merely by shouting loudly enough. Facing up to reality – as finite humans must – means facing up to the reality of your moods, desires, and interests, too. This is why it takes courage to ask yourself the question that I suspect all those gurus promoting the 'warrior mindset' and 'mental toughness' are too frightened to ask themselves: How would you like to spend your time today?

Don't stand in generosity's way

On the futility of 'becoming a better person'

'Everybody loves something. Even if it's just tortillas.'

— CHÖGYAM TRUNGPA

Many of us believe we ought to be kinder or more generous, to give more money to charity, spend more time volunteering, or in some vaguer way 'become a better person' than we currently are. The Tibetan Buddhist master Chögyam Trungpa's point is that this isn't necessary: you needn't try to transform yourself into someone who feels more love for humanity, and it's probably impossible anyway. You just need to find where you already feel warmth or tenderness, then go from there. And your penchant for Mexican food is as good a place to start as any other.

In truth, there's a debate to be had about how good a person Chögyam Trungpa himself was. An alcoholic who once crashed a car into a joke shop in north-east England (every word of that is true), he could be deeply obnoxious to his followers; and over the last few years, the Shambhala spiritual movement that he founded has been rocked by allegations of sexual misconduct against his son, who succeeded him as leader. Still, in this case, I think his point stands. Being a better or more loving person is another thing you can't make happen. You have to let it happen – which you can do by first recognizing that some part of you already feels the emotions you believe you ought to be feeling. After that, your main job is to avoid overcomplicating things.

Obviously, I don't know you, so I suppose it's possible that you *are* a malevolent weasel who actively wishes harm on your fellow men and women. But if you're the kind of person who worries that they might be deficient in generosity or kindness, it's far more likely that you have all sorts of generous thoughts and impulses, all the time, and that your problem – if you're anything like me – is that you repeatedly fail to do very much about them. Or to be more precise: you inadvertently erect obstacles to action. A homeless person asks you for money, and you have some change, and you feel moved to help – but then you recall how you've always been told it's far more effective to donate to a well-run homelessness charity instead, so you resolve to do this, but then never quite get around to it. Or you think of something you'd love to say to a friend with whom you've fallen out of touch, but you're tired right now, and that kind of email deserves doing properly, so you postpone it. Or you'd like to help out at the school fair, but this is an especially busy period, so it makes sense to get on top of your to-do list first, then aim to help out at the next one.

None of these cases indicates any profound deficiency in your character. Nothing was wrong with your essential impulses. It's just that for the usual perfectionistic, limit-denying reasons – wanting to be *optimally* kind instead of just kind, or wanting to feel in full control of your time and obligations – you never managed to translate your impulses into action.

This is why I can wholeheartedly recommend a personal policy I learned from the (vastly less problematic) meditation teacher Joseph Goldstein, and that I seek to follow myself, which is to act on a generous impulse the moment it arises. The point isn't to try to render yourself more generous than you already are, but just to notice the moments when you naturally and effortlessly feel that way anyway, then not to screw it up with overthinking. The simplest way to do that is to move fast. 'Each time the thought to give arises, act on it. Then notice what happens,' Goldstein counsels, adding that 'in my experience, generosity never leads to remorse.' What happens, unsurprisingly, is that it feels great, so while initiating the practice can require a little willpower, it soon becomes self-reinforcing. Before you know it, you're a person who acts more generously – without ever having had to become a more generous person.

And in any case, wasn't there always something a little conceptually confused about your desire to 'become a better person'? All else aside, the fact that you felt the desire in the first place suggests that you already possessed the values you were chastising yourself for lacking; only someone with morals can beat themselves up for lacking morals. (Does anyone imagine that Vladimir Putin lies awake at night, worrying if he's really as caring and thoughtful a person as he'd like to believe?) And when this sort of confusion is your starting point, trying to change your personality can only end in a circular, self-absorbed tangle of guilt and obligation. Which, incidentally, does nothing to help other people. Far better to locate the generosity that's already inside you, then be sure not to get in its way.

Allow other people their problems

On minding your own business

'People-pleasing is a form of assholery ... because you're not pleasing anybody – you're just making them resentful because you're being disingenuous, and you're also not giving them the dignity of their own experience [by assuming] they can't handle the truth.'

— WHITNEY CUMMINGS

'Great news! I found the cure for my anxiety!!' the author Sarah Gailey once announced on social media. 'All I need is for everyone I know to tell me definitively that they aren't mad at me, once every fifteen seconds, forever.' I know how she feels. For years, I possessed a remarkable super-power: I could turn any work opportunity, no matter how exciting or delightful, into an unpleasant emotional drama, simply by agreeing to do it. Once I'd accepted a deadline or signed a contract, there was another person in the world who might be growing impatient that I hadn't finished yet, or who might be disappointed with what I produced – and the thought of their harboring any negativity towards me felt hugely oppressive. The same overinvestment in other people's emotions meant I was always saying yes to things I should have declined, because I flinched internally at the thought of the other person being crestfallen. And that I rarely fully enjoyed myself at social gatherings, thanks to a suspicion that the others present, however happy they seemed, might only reluctantly be spending time with me.

What I eventually figured out – not that it ever seems to get particularly easy – is that other people's negative emotions are ultimately a problem that belongs to them. And you have to allow other people their problems. This is one more area in which the best thing to do, as a finite human with limited control, is usually not to meddle, but to let things be.

Before we go any further, it bears emphasizing that the people you're worried might be angry with you or bored by you or disappointed in you almost never are. They've got their own troubles to worry about. According to stereotype, people-pleasers are self-effacing types, and yet there's something strikingly grandiose about the notion that your boss, client or coworker has nothing better to do than pace up and down all day thinking bad thoughts about *you* – or that your presence at a social gathering has the power to ruin it for anyone else. 'It's weird how when I don't respond to someone's email, it's because I'm busy,' observes the novelist Leila

Sales, poking fun at this tendency in herself, 'but when other people don't respond to my emails, it's because they hate me.' (It's worth noting, too, that on the mercifully few occasions that an adult actually *has* exploded in rage at me, it had never occurred to me for a moment that they might be angry. Clearly, I'd been worrying about the wrong people.)

But what if someone genuinely is furious, disappointed, or otherwise upset with you? Still – at the most fundamental level – not your problem. I'm not endorsing the 'ignore the haters!' mentality you sometimes encounter from self-help gurus, according to which you should ignore other people's emotions as a matter of principle. Nor is it carte blanche to be a jerk to others, treating them like dirt before sauntering away, complacently reassuring yourself that you needn't take responsibility for the feelings you just triggered. Instead, the point is simply that it's a fool's errand – and a flagrant denial of your finite power over reality – to make your sense of feeling OK dependent on knowing that everyone around you is feeling OK, too.

Taken at face value, the news that somebody is upset because you're not behaving as they wanted you to behave is just that: a report on the state of their emotional weather. You might or might not choose to act on such a report, but that's an entirely separate matter. Every decision is a question of trade-offs, as we saw on Day Three, and other people's emotions are one more thing to be weighed in the balance. Your cantankerous manager is bugging you for a reply to his email, or your anxious partner wants you to hurry up and make a decision on your travel plans: in either case, you might decide it's in your best interests, or in keeping with your values, to act promptly – and if you do, your outward behavior will be the same as if you'd been motivated by a cringing desire to assuage their distress. But the full reality of the situation will be very different. You'll be making a conscious choice, weighing their emotions against your other priorities. Alternatively, in either scenario, you might decide this is one of those times they're going to have to handle their feelings without your help.

One of the main reasons we fail to treat other people's emotions in this clear-headed way is that they sail under the flag of 'urgency.' Some tasks are legitimately time-sensitive, of course; but the unpleasant anxiety that attaches itself to tasks we've deemed 'urgent' is often a sign that someone else's priorities are in control. The sense of urgency is really the fear that someone else will get angry or anxious if you don't hurry up. Again, maybe it's in your interests to forestall that outcome. But then again, maybe it isn't: their feelings have no magic power to reach out and force you to act. It might help to consider the billions of people on earth who are, at this moment, feeling angry, depressed, disappointed, impatient, or anxious. The thought of them might evoke your sympathy; yet you surely don't see it as your job to cheer them all up. Why should it automatically be different in that small proportion of cases where the emotions are, at least nominally, about you?

But the real revelation, as Whitney Cummings says, is that people-pleasing isn't even an especially effective way of pleasing other people. Going through life trying to placate them doesn't make you fun to work or live with. People pick up on the fact that you're treating them with kid gloves, and only fulfilling your commitments to them in an effort to make yourself feel better, rather than being honestly motivated by a desire to help, so they feel patronized or manipulated – or just annoyed at having to dedicate any brain-space at all to your personal issues. Sometimes, your agonizing actively complicates their lives. 'You know,' a *Guardian* editor once told me, very early in my career, after she'd been waiting all day for me to tell her whether or not I could take on a certain assignment, because I feared I didn't have the bandwidth, yet also couldn't bear to disappoint her, 'if you can't do something, saying no right away usually makes it much easier for everyone.'

It was years before it struck me that this might have been one of the most generous things anyone had ever said to me. It helped me see that if trying so hard to manage other people's emotions wasn't even helping *them*, I had less to lose by abandoning the endeavor. And so I began to grapple with a truth that people-pleasers are prone to resist until it halfway kills them: that very often, the best way to benefit others is to focus on doing your thing.

A good time or a good story

On the upsides of unpredictability

'It helps if you can realize that this part of life when you don't know what's coming is often the part that people look back on with the greatest affection.'

— ANN PATCHETT

I t's possible I've given the impression, so far, that the lack of control you have over how reality unfolds is just one of those unfortunate truths to which you'd better resign yourself. But it's more than that. In some profound way, it's a *good* thing. Not being able to guarantee that your plans will come off; not knowing what the future holds; never quite feeling like you've got things figured out, or that you're on top of things – all of these are mysteriously central to what makes life worth living.

Bear with me on this one.

Almost everything that happens, according to an adage of uncertain origin, is either a good time or a good story. Either things go right, or they go wrong; and surprisingly often when they do go wrong – although of course not invariably – life ends up unaccountably better as a result. A friend I've known since we were teenagers treasures the memory of one weekend when her mother and father drove her and her sisters to the countryside for a picnic. Just as they'd laid an impressive lunch spread on the blanket, the heavens opened, but on this occasion, the parents let the kids eat anyway, in a pandemonium of wet sandwiches and laughter. These days, it's a glowing gem among her recollections of childhood – and what makes that so interesting, to me, is how utterly unexceptional it is. Plenty of straightforwardly undesirable things happen to all of us, from the mildly annoying to the tragic. But almost everyone, when prompted, can reel off a few tales in which events slipped out of their control – the weather failed to cooperate, the flight got canceled, they showed up at the wrong address – and either something wonderful happened or, at worst, they acquired an anecdote with which to entertain themselves and others for years to come.

If conducting scores of newspaper interviews with minor celebrities taught me anything, it's that this same inverse relationship between control and gratification crops up across the whole of a life. Ask people to relate the milestones of their biography, and they'll almost always dwell on moments whose consequences they could never have anticipated. They might mention a period of despair they'd have avoided entirely, if they could possibly have done so, such as a struggle with addiction, or a terrifying diagnosis; or else some seemingly mundane incident that proved pivotal, like the party at which they met their future spouse, or the dashed-off email that unexpectedly landed them a job. In *Four Thousand Weeks*, I quoted the philosopher Simone de Beauvoir tracing the idea still further back, to the astonishing fact that she was ever born in the first place: 'The penetration of that particular ovum by that particular spermatozoon, with its implications of the meeting of my parents and before that of their birth and the birth of all their forebears, had not one chance in hundreds of millions of coming about.'

And yet despite the strange benefits that so often seem to arise from our lack of control, we proceed through life – as individuals, but as societies, too – as if the supreme goal should be always and only to obtain more and more of it. 'The driving cultural force of that form of life we call "modern" is the idea, the hope and desire, that we can make the world *controllable*,' writes Hartmut Rosa, the German social theorist we met in the introduction. In his magnum opus *Resonance*, and a follow-up work, *The Uncontrollability of the World*, Rosa shows how all kinds of disparate human endeavors fit together when understood as attempts to do that very thing. The quest to dominate nature; progress in medicine; the growth of military power; digital connectivity, which lets us keep abreast of what's happening thousands of miles away, and air travel, which brings far-off places within reach;

helicopter parenting, dieting, in-vitro fertilization, Elon Musk's proposed colonization of Mars, lab-grown meat: all are plausibly motivated by the human need to feel more in control than before.

Rosa certainly doesn't deny that the quest for controllability has brought incalculable benefits; after all, it's behind virtually everything that makes life today so much freer from unremitting poverty and pain than it was in medieval times. And he's clear he's not arguing that underprivileged people should reconcile themselves to having less control over their lives than wealthier ones. But he shows that, simultaneously, our desire for controllability backfires, undermining our efforts to build happy and fulfilling lives. The human domination of nature has caused nature to escape human control, threatening our flourishing through runaway climate disruption. The more people with whom we're able to connect digitally, the worse the loneliness epidemic gets; and the more vigilance parents exert over their children's comfort, the more anxious and uncomfortable they are.

In short, the more we try to render the world controllable, the more it eludes us; and the more daily life loses what Rosa calls its resonance, its capacity to touch, move and absorb us. As soon as any experience can be completely controlled, it feels cold and dead; a work of art you fully understand or a person whose behavior you can predict with total accuracy is no fun at all. What brings fulfillment is being in a certain form of reciprocal relationship with the rest of the world, including other people; you might liken it to a dance in which you alternately lead and follow.

Whereas a relationship in which you unquestionably have the upper hand at all times is no relationship at all.

On a societal level, the quest for control often directly undermines our capacity to do meaningful work. If you're a teacher or a social worker, if you work in academia or health-care or the charity sector, or if you're close to somebody in any of these roles, you'll be familiar with how virtually every-one in such fields complains about barely having time to do their jobs, these days, thanks to all the admin involved in doing their jobs. That paperwork results from their employ-ers' efforts to render the processes of their work controllable, by making it transparent and measurable. Yet the result is that they have far fewer opportunities to create the unpre-dictable moments of human connection in which the real work gets done. 'The blight of having to make everything controllable,' writes Rosa, 'has everywhere infected the uncontrollable productivity of social life.'

The point is a subtle one, he notes, because a resonant relationship with life depends on its being *semi*-controllable, not totally uncontrollable. You need to engage actively in the world – to connect to others, to make plans, and to pursue opportunities and ambitions – and people need the freedom, and the economic resources, to be able to do that. (Neither good times nor good stories will occur very often if you just sit around, isolated, waiting for them – or if you're obliged to spend every waking hour struggling to survive.) Still, it's central to an enjoyable and meaningful life that whenever we reach out to the world in this way, we don't get to control how it responds. The value and depth of the experience relies on that unknowability. Maybe you'll get what you wanted, or maybe you won't – and sometimes, not getting what you wanted will leave life immeasurably better.

There's an inadvertently amusing moment in James Wagner's English translation of *Resonance*, in a passage where Rosa seeks to clarify precisely the feeling evoked by this sort of relationship to reality. The book is a weighty academic work, with forty pages of footnotes, and many references to obscure scholars. But when Rosa reaches for the perfect adjective to describe this feeling of both acting on the world and being acted on by it, engaging with it boldly yet never knowing how it will respond – and the feelings of warmth and fulfillment that result – the term he chooses is *anschmieg-samen*. What *anschmiegsamen* means in English – and this is the word that appears, startlingly yet wonderfully, in the translated version of the passage – is 'cuddly.'

Set a quantity goal

On firing your inner quality controller

'There is neither a proportional relationship, nor an inverse one, between a writer's estimation of a work in progress and its actual quality. The feeling that the work is magnificent, and the feeling that it is abominable, are both mosquitoes to be repelled, ignored, or killed, but not indulged.'

— ANNIE DILLARD

One more paradoxical truth about control: often, the way to have the best ideas, and to produce the best work, is to develop an ability to forget entirely about trying to control the quality of your output. And the easiest way to do *that* is to focus on quantity instead.

('Quantity has a quality all its own,' as someone once said, though there's an uncomfortable possibility that it may have been Joseph Stalin.)

In York in northern England, where I grew up, the ancient walls that encircle the city are punctuated at four main points by gatehouses known as bars, which these days mainly contribute to traffic jams, but which were originally used to keep a close watch on people attempting to enter the city, or to lock it down entirely in case of attack. I imagine a lithe Roman guard or portly Viking, operating the heavy wooden portcullis that once blocked each gate, interrogating would-be visitors and then, only if satisfied with the answers received, grudgingly raising the barrier to admit them, before swiftly slamming it shut again. I can't vouch for the historical accuracy of this image. But it's the metaphor I've always liked for how control-seeking people – which is to say most of us, to one degree or another – tend to treat our work. We operate on the assumption that any idea we come up with probably won't be good enough, so we subject it to the scrutiny of a beady-eyed inner gatekeeper, and only reluctantly, if it first meets the gatekeeper's stringent standards, allow it out on to the screen, or the page, or into the brainstorming meeting.

What this looks like in my line of work is staring at a screen, slowly and painstakingly formulating half a sentence, reading it over, deeming it to be inadequate, deleting it, staring at the screen some more, then trying again. (As the writing coach Stephen Lloyd Webber points out, it's ironic that people call this process 'writing,' since the vast majority of it entails not writing, or deleting things you've just written.) And the situation spirals, because each time you finally permit something on to the page, its imperfections dismay you so much that you tighten the quality criteria further still – until, to switch metaphors unpleasantly, you're so constipated no words can squeeze their way out at all.

This is the point at which a certain kind of self-styled creative person starts talking vaguely about 'falling in love with the process.' I've done it myself. Since it's so agonizing to produce good work, the thinking goes, why not delight in the simple fact of working instead? But these days I'm fairly sure this is usually a defense mechanism, deployed by people who feel anxious about the eventual result of their efforts – and that it never really works, anyway, because if it's just a fact that you do care about the outcome, telling yourself you don't isn't going to help. 'In a conversation I had with a friend recently,' the splendidly crotchety creativity expert Robert Fritz writes in his book *The Path of Least Resistance*, 'she talked about "the sacredness of process" and "transcendental appreciation of one's process." I could almost hear a choir of angels softly singing as she rhapsodized.' Besides, this sort of talk is only really tolerated among arty types: try telling the customers of your accountancy practice or law firm you've decided to focus on 'loving the process,' not filing their taxes or drawing up their wills, and see where it gets you.

A more pragmatic and imperfectionist way to ease up on a fixation with outcomes is to set a quantity goal. There's no need to pretend you don't care about the results of your work, or to eradicate the part of you that seeks control. Give that part something to do – just make sure it has nothing to do with the quality of the result. Eight hundred words per day;

one hour on the side business every evening; five potential customers contacted; three pages of the material for the examination turned into flashcards (or the three-hour rule we encountered on Day Thirteen): these are goals anyone with the available time can achieve, so long as you're willing to accept that, for now, quality isn't the point. The entrepreneur James Altucher suggests a daily practice of writing down ten ideas, about whatever seems compelling, on a notepad: ten people to reach out to, ten possible plans for the weekend, ten ways to make money, etcetera. What if you can't think of ten? 'Here's the magic trick: if you can't come up with ten ideas, come up with twenty ideas.' Quantity overpowers perfectionism, as Altucher explains: 'Perfectionism is your brain trying to protect you from harm. From coming up with an idea that is embarrassing and stupid and could cause you to suffer pain. We like the brain. But you have to shut the brain off to come up with ideas.' A quantity goal puts you back in the driver's seat: instead of *hoping* you produce something good, you get to know you'll produce *something*.

The alternative to the stare-at-the-screen approach to writing is 'freewriting,' in which you set a time-based quantity goal – ten minutes, say – then write, without stopping, until your timer goes off. (In no way is this technique only useful for professional writers: you can use it to write about any professional or personal challenge you're facing.) The point isn't to hurry to generate as many words as you can; writing slowly is fine, so long as you don't stop. The real point is to upend the standard arrangement in which your main activity, while staring at the screen or the page, is 'thinking of something to write,' and only actually writing something if the gatekeeper deigns to let it through. In freewriting, you fire the gatekeeper, jam the portcullis open, and write regardless of whether or not you've got anything to write. (If you can't think of anything to write about, write about that.)

Need I say that I hated freewriting at first? Allowing one's ideas on to the screen with no quality control violates everything the uptight perfectionist stands for, even though you can always edit or delete it later. Still, the method surprises me, over and over. Sometimes because it leads to good writing or creative solutions, and at other times because it reminds me that when my output falls wildly short of my standards – when the writing's no good, or no creative solution presents itself – the world never actually seems to collapse.

DAY TWENTY-ONE

What's an interruption, anyway?

On the importance of staying distractible

'The great thing, if one can, is to stop regarding all the unpleasant things as interruptions of one's "own," or "real" life. The truth is of course that what one calls the interruptions are precisely one's real life – the life God is sending one day by day.'

— C. S. LEWIS

You might be convinced you'd have no struggle making time for what counts if only other people would leave you alone, or if you weren't so easily distracted. But this turns out to be one last context in which, as we've seen throughout this week, it's often a good idea to ease up on exerting control. Even interruptions and distractions can be among those things it's wisest to let happen.

Anyone with even a passing interest in personal productivity will have tried, at some point, to tame interruptions and distraction by means of techniques like 'time-boxing,' in which you decide in advance which tasks you'll complete during each hour of the day, or 'focus rituals' to help you master your attention and resist mind-wandering, or just by hiding in some corner of your home or workplace where there's less chance of being disturbed. But if you've done so, you've probably also discovered the perverse consequences of such interventions, which are a) that they tend to make interruptions and distractions feel worse, when they do happen; and b) that they cause more things to get defined as unwelcome interruptions in the first place. Suppose it's 4.10 p.m., on a day when it's not my turn for school pickup, and I'm focusing hard in my office at home when my son bursts in, to tell me excitedly of his preparations for the school play. A small moment of connection, the kind of thing life's supposed to be about – except that if my time-boxing plan deems 4 p.m. to 5 p.m. an hour for deep focus, then his entrance is suddenly an intrusion, one more minor way in which my day has gone wrong. Had I spent the five minutes prior to 4 p.m. doing a focus meditation, entering a state of mental quiet in preparation for my hour of concentration, his arrival would be still more jarring and unwelcome.

On a larger scale, you can fall into the trap of viewing your whole life this way, interpreting all the things you're actually doing with your days as one extended series of interruptions or distractions from what you think you're *meant* to be doing with them. Of course you might legitimately dislike certain aspects of your job, or your life. But going through the world with the default belief that it's full of people or things that need holding at bay is a self-fulfilling prophecy. It makes ever more people and things feel like they must indeed be held at bay, if you're ever to get a moment to hear yourself think.

Next time you do get a moment to hear yourself think, though, you could use it to ponder the strange assumption of omniscience that's baked into the notion of minimizing 'interruptions' and blocking out 'distractions.' The idea that these labels can confidently be applied to things before they happen implies that you always know, in advance, the best way for any portion of your time to unfold – and that should reality beg to differ, it must always be reality that's wrong. And yet, objectively, all that's occurring in the world is that certain things happen, then other things happen, then still more things happen. When we define some of these things as interruptions of, or distractions from, other ones, we're adding a mental overlay to the situation, sorting events into hard categories of those which ought and ought not to happen. There's nothing intrinsically wrong with that; it's fine to have strong preferences for how you'd like your day to unfold. But at the very least, it's a reminder not to cling so confidently to those preferences that you turn life into a constant struggle against events you've decided, futilely, shouldn't be happening. Or that you close off the possibility that what looks like an interruption might in fact prove a welcome development.

As the Zen teacher John Tarrant explains, the way we talk about distraction implies something equally unhelpful: a model of the human mind according to which its default state is one of stability, steadiness and single-pointed focus. 'Telling myself I'm distracted,' he writes, 'is a way of yanking on the leash and struggling to get back to equilibrium.' But the truth is that fixity of attention isn't our baseline. The natural state of the mind is often for it to bounce gently around, usually remaining only loosely focused and receptive to new stimuli, the state sometimes known as 'open awareness,' which neuroscientific research has shown is associated with incubating creativity. There are sound evolutionary reasons why this should be the case: the prehistoric human who could choose to fix her attention firmly on one thing, and leave it there for hours on end, so that nothing could disturb her, would soon have been devoured by a saber-toothed tiger. Monks in some traditions spend years developing single-pointed focus, in monasteries expressly designed to provide the required seclusion, precisely because it *doesn't* come naturally. And so where the idea of interruption defines unanticipated external events as inherently bad, the idea of distraction defines the movements of the mind as similarly problematic.

Going through life with a rigid commitment to the elimination of interruption and distraction might seem like a way to stay more absorbed in what's happening. Yet in fact it pulls you out of it, by undermining your capacity to respond to reality as it actually unfolds – to seize unexpected opportunities and to be seized by an awe-inspiring landscape or fascinating conversation; to let your mind take an unplanned journey into fertile creative territory, or to find enjoyment, as opposed to annoyance, in a small child bursting into your study, while fulfilling your obligations as a parent. 'Getting lost and distracted in this way is what life is for,' Tarrant writes. Looking at things from this angle, you might even argue that what makes modern digital distraction so pernicious isn't the way it disrupts attention, but the fact that it *holds* it, with content algorithmically engineered to compel people for hours, thereby rendering them less available for the serendipitous and fruitful kind of distraction.

None of this means you shouldn't have boundaries, or try to work somewhere quiet, or that you must welcome every instance of pestering by every oblivious or entitled jerk in your life. It might just mean approaching the phenomena we pejoratively label 'interruptions' and 'distractions' a little more neutrally. Paul Loomans (who we met on Day Eleven, about 'just going to the shed') calls them 'drop-ins.' His advice is to give them your full attention. That is: once your focus has already been diverted – once the child has burst into the room, or the anxious thought about the timing of your doctor's appointment has pulled you away from the novel you were reading – don't fight the fact. Deal with your new reality instead. Make a note to check the time of the appointment; or look the child in the eyes, listen to their request – then either close your laptop to be with them, or explain you'll need to finish what you're doing first. It's entirely possible, Loomans notes, 'to give someone your undivided attention while telling them you don't have time right now,' and far more pleasant for all involved than attempting to keep part of your focus on whatever it was you were just doing. When you try that, 'you get tense and the other person doesn't feel heard. They might even stay longer and keep pressing their point.'

And speaking of children bursting into rooms: at the time of writing, almost 60 million people have watched the moment during the coronavirus pandemic when the two small children of Robert Kelly, an expert on Korean politics based in Busan in South Korea, entered the study where he was giving a live interview to the BBC and capered wildly for several seconds, before his wife acrobatically managed to extract them. Is anyone seriously going to claim this interruption turned out to be a bad thing? Obviously not: it made a strange moment in history microscopically more joyful, and kindled empathy worldwide from locked-down parents struggling to juggle work and family. 'We thought no TV network would ever call us again,' Kelly recalled later, but the opposite proved the case; it was professionally beneficial, too. You can never tell in advance. We try so hard to cling to the rock face of fixed focus; we fall off, again and again – yet when we do, as Tarrant beautifully puts it, 'the world catches us every time.' We lose our grip on our plans for the day, and find ourselves tumbling into life.

Week Four

Showing Up

'The story comes from China, and tells of an old painter who invited friends to see his newest picture. This picture showed a park and a narrow footpath that ran along a stream and through a grove of trees, culminating at the door of a little cottage in the background. When the painter's friends, however, looked around for the painter, they saw that he had left them – that he was in the picture. There, he followed the little path that led to the door, paused before it quite still, turned, smiled, and disappeared through the narrow opening. In the same way, I too, when occupied with my paintpots and brushes, would be suddenly displaced into the picture. I would resemble the porcelain which I had entered in a cloud of colours.'

— WALTER BENJAMIN

Stop being so kind to Future You

On entering time and space completely

'[There is a] strange attitude and feeling that one is *not yet* in real life. For the time being, one is doing this or that, but whether it is [a relationship with] a woman or a job, it is *not yet* what is really wanted, and there is always the fantasy that sometime in the future the real thing will come about ... The one thing dreaded throughout by such a type of man is to be bound to anything whatever. There is a terrific fear of being pinned down, of entering time and space completely, and of being the singular human being that one is.'

— MARIE-LOUISE VON FRANZ

If there's a single truth at the heart of the imperfectionist outlook, it's the one to which we turn as we begin this final week: that this, here and now, is real life. This is it. This portion of your limited time, the part *before* you've managed to get on top of everything, or dealt with your procrastination problem, or graduated or found a partner or retired; and before the survival of democracy or the climate have been secured: this part matters just as much as any other and arguably even more than any other, since the past is gone and the future hasn't occurred yet, so right now is the only time that really exists. If instead you take the other approach – if you see all of this as leading up to some future point when real life will begin, or when you can finally start enjoying yourself, or feeling good about yourself – then you'll end up treating your actual life as something to 'get through,' until one day it'll be over, without the meaningful part ever having arrived. We have to show up as fully as possible here, in the swim of things as they are. None of that means you don't get to harbor ambitious plans as well – about the things you'll accomplish, the fortune you'll accumulate, or the difference you'll make to the world. Far from it. It means you get to pursue those goals *and* feel alive and absorbed while pursuing them, instead of postponing the aliveness to when or if they're achieved.

When she wrote the haunting passage quoted above, the Swiss psychologist and scholar of fairy tales Marie-Louise von Franz had in mind a certain kind of adult, more often a man, who clings to a commitment-free existence because he's scared of the sacrifices entailed by taking life more seriously. He can be a charming sort of person to be around, until one day he very much isn't, and he's suddenly the dubious fifty-something in a bar full of 25-year-olds, having frittered his real future away on fantasies of an unlimited one. But there's another way to end up living what von Franz called 'the provisional life,' which is, in a sense, to take life *too* seriously: to obsess so much about using your time wisely or efficiently for future purposes that you find yourself treating the present as mere preparation for the stage when you'll have everything running smoothly. This is the fate of the person that John Maynard Keynes described as 'the purposive man,' who 'does not love his cat, but his cat's kittens; nor, in truth, the kittens, but only the kittens' kittens, and so on forward forever to the end of cat-dom.'

The philosopher Dean Rickles has written poignantly of his own struggles with the second sort of provisional life. At twelve, he recalls, he was struck by 'an absolute epiphany': the idea 'that I could spare my future self trouble and make the future better by acting a specific way' in the present. And so he got down to work. Among the various methods by which he made himself miserable so as to be happy later, he practiced piano so aggressively that he split his fingertips open. He took deferring gratification to an extreme. The strategy of treating life as an exercise in doing favors for his future self 'served me well in some ways, but very badly in others, since I engaged in the practice to a punishing degree from which I'm still recovering . . . Pretty bloody pathological, and utterly shocking, bizarre behavior in retrospect.' Back then, he'd assumed his future self would thank him; but these days, he writes, what he mainly feels for his past self is pity.

It's not that concern for one's future self is entirely bad, especially when you're young. You can argue that it's easy for Rickles to regret his past self-punishment now that he's already an accomplished pianist – just as it's easy for me to say I wish I hadn't made myself sick with anxiety studying for my university degree, now that I've built a career that may not have been open to me without it. But no less than in the case of von Franz's commitment-phobe, the motive for caring too much about one's future self is the horror of being finite. For simplicity's sake, I'm describing these as two distinct personality types, but many of us will have elements of both. I know I do.

The commitment-phobe can't bear to enter 'time and space completely' because letting himself be pinned down to one relationship or career path means renouncing the other ones. He imagines that what he's doing instead is keeping his options open, though he has of course chosen a path – because choosing to use up some of your finite time in a state of non-commitment is still a choice. On the other hand, the too-responsible type holds off from entering time and space completely by always locating the real value of her present-day actions somewhere off in the future. This allows her to experience what Keynes called 'a spurious and delusive immortality,' following the cock-eyed logic that if the point of your life is coming later, it must be the case that you'll still be alive to experience it – so that as long as you continue investing in your future, maybe you won't have to die.

According to one popular strain of self-help advice, the only viable alternative to living in the future in this manner is to 'live in the moment' in a way that entails renouncing big plans and taking things easy, exerting yourself no more than might be required to travel to your next yoga retreat. Really, though, showing up more fully in the present is about *how* you pursue your plans for the future; it certainly doesn't require that you abandon them. It means letting go of the notion that you can't quite allow yourself to feel fully immersed in life before those plans are realized, and coming to understand on the contrary that the pursuit of ambitious goals is one excellent *way* to be fully immersed in life. (Looking back, I see that I was always telling myself that once I figured out how to be a national newspaper journalist, or a good partner, or the best possible parent, I'd let myself relax into those roles; now, at least on my better days, I realize that the activity of figuring such things out is the substance of an absorbing life, not something I need to do in order to prepare for one.)

Then again, while entering the present more fully needn't necessarily mean taking things easy, it's entirely possible that in your case it might. Perhaps it's time for a sabbatical, or for what Tim Ferriss calls a 'mini-retirement,' an intentional break in which you undertake, now, one of the adventures you were mentally deferring until much later in life. After all, there's never any guarantee that you'll still be around to do it years in the future. At the very least, it might be time to spend an hour today enjoying yourself – cashing in some of the investments you previously made in your future self, you might say, and splashing out on the present one.

We all know there are plenty of people who might benefit from learning to defer gratification much more than they currently do. It's just that if you're the kind of person who vigorously agrees with that statement, it's highly likely that you'd benefit from learning to defer it less. You're probably familiar with the so-called 'marshmallow experiments,' in which the social psychologist Walter Mischel and his colleagues presented children with a single marshmallow and offered them a choice: they could eat it, or wait alone in the room with it for ten minutes, in which case they'd get one more. In footage of some versions of the experiment, the dutiful gratification-deferrers sing or talk to themselves out loud, in an effort to overrule their urge to eat the marshmallow in front of them. Participants who were able to resist temptation went on to enjoy better academic performance and physical health in later childhood, and to demonstrate other positive differences as adults. The reasons are still debated – but it seems clear that the self-discipline not to grab the first marshmallow is an invaluable trait for what's commonly thought of as a successful life. On the other hand, there's no virtue in accumulating the greatest number of uneaten marshmallows that would be delicious were you ever to let yourself consume one. At some point, in order to experience the benefits of having received any in the first place, you're going to have to eat a damn marshmallow.

DAY TWENTY-THREE

How to start from sanity

On paying yourself first

'To treat life as a pilgrimage to a future and better existence is to disown its present value.'

— W. SOMERSET MAUGHAM

One conclusion that follows from the fact that *this is it* is that striving towards sanity is never going to work. You have to operate from sanity instead. This is liable to sound a bit cryptic, but the practical implications are huge.

I'm using 'sanity' here to refer, very broadly, to what it feels like to live the kind of life you want to be living – which in my case means calm and focused, energetic and meaningfully productive, and connected to others, as opposed to anxious, isolated and overwhelmed. To me, above all, the word evokes an essential sense of groundedness, persisting even through times of difficulty or unpleasantness. Yet unless you consider your existence to be completely perfect already, it's natural to treat the state of sanity as something you're working towards. You probably have a bit of it, but you'd like to have much more; being, for example, non-overwhelmed is a place you hope to get to, later on. That place might feel like it's just around the corner, or very far away; but the point is that it's not the place you're starting from. It's somewhere else.

And yet it appears to be a fundamental rule that if you treat sanity as a state you have to reach by engaging in all manner of preparations, or getting other things out of the way first, then the main effect will be to reinforce the sense of sanity as something that's out of reach. You'll entrench the stress and anxiety, rather than uprooting them. You might get all sorts of useful things done – but they'll never bring peace of mind, because you'll effectively be telling yourself on a daily basis that peace of mind is something distant and not available right here.

That's what I mean by 'striving towards sanity.' 'Operating from sanity,' on the other hand, means embodying a certain kind of orientation towards life first, one that treats the present moment as a place where peace of mind might, in theory, be attainable – and then going about your life from that orientation, rather than treating the activities of your life as things you're doing in order to one day reach it. In his book *Anti-Time Management*, Richie Norton boils this philosophy down to two steps. One: 'Decide who you want to be.' Two: 'Act from that identity immediately.'

The signature behavior of the striver-towards-sanity is

'clearing the decks': trying to deal with all the minor tasks tugging at your attention in an effort to arrive at the point when you finally expect to have large stretches of time to focus on what you care about. The trouble with clearing the decks, as we've seen, is that the supply of things to fill the decks is to all intents and purposes limitless. So a commitment to clearing the decks leads inexorably to a life spent unendingly clearing the decks.

The signature behavior of the operator-from-sanity, by contrast, is what the creativity coach Jessica Abel calls 'paying yourself first with time': spending a little time on what matters to you most immediately, instead of waiting, because you understand that even thirty minutes spent Actually Doing the Thing today are more valuable than hundreds of purely hypothetical hours in the future. Similarly, while the striver-towards-sanity who's feeling exhausted might end up grinding harder – making life less restful now, in hope of making relaxation possible later – the operator-from-sanity realizes she'd better pause to rest today, however briefly.

Of course, you might not *feel* calm or undistracted or 'sane' while you're doing any of this, especially at first. Apart from anything else, you might feel acutely anxious about the uncleared decks you're ignoring. But the point of operating from sanity is to engage in the behaviors that constitute a meaningful life anyway, and to allow the feelings to follow, rather than spending your life scrambling fruitlessly after the feelings. There are three especially useful techniques to bear in mind here:

Deal with a backlog by isolating it. If you've accumulated an unpleasant backlog of email or other small tasks, striving towards sanity might entail setting aside five whole days to do nothing but plow through all of it – which is unlikely to work, partly because you won't maintain the motivation, and also because other tasks and messages will accumulate in the meantime, leaving you no less backlogged than before. Operating from sanity, when it comes to backlogs, means following the advice of the time management expert Mark Forster instead. First, sequester all those emails in a separate folder, or the tasks on a separate to-do list. (And just like that, your inbox is empty!) Thereafter, your priority isn't to blast through the backlog, but to stay up to date on *new* incoming emails or tasks, so as to prevent another backlog developing. Chip away at the old one a little per day – or, if you think you can get away with it, just forget about it entirely.

Free up time by renegotiating existing commitments, not just planning to make fewer. If what stands between you and peace of mind is a whole lot of commitments you wish you'd never made, striving towards sanity would involve attempting to meet them all, while firmly resolving to make fewer new commitments from here on. (Spoiler alert: you'll make just as many as before.) Operating from sanity, in this case, means biting the bullet and renegotiating some of the commitments that are *already* on your plate: backing out of projects, requesting deadline extensions, or canceling social plans, so as to reduce the real, current demands on your time, not just hypothetical demands on it later.

Treat your to-do list as a menu. In the striving-towards-sanity mindset, a to-do list is always something you've got to get to the end of before you're allowed to relax. But in any context where there are more things that feel like they need doing than there's time available in which to do them – which is the normal state of affairs, after all – a to-do list is by definition really a menu, a list of tasks to pick from, rather than to get through. And operating from sanity means treating it that way: starting with the acknowledgment that you won't complete everything you might wish, then making your selections from the menu. Obviously, not every task on every to-do list will be as appetizing as the restaurant analogy suggests. But it's surprising how many things do become more appetizing once you're encountering them not as chores you have to plow through, but as options you get to pick.

Operating from sanity, as I mentioned, can feel awkward at first. Yet beneath the awkwardness, there's often almost immediately a strange new kind of satisfaction. You feel more engrossed in your experience, and like you're exerting more influence over the world, even though you've achieved that by relaxing rather than intensifying your attempts to feel in control of it. Life certainly doesn't become problem-free and, what's more, you're no longer so confident it ever will. But your problems start to feel more tractable and interesting, and often enough you find you can approach them with relish. This way of being feels less like lying on a beach in the sun and more like striding over hills, with the wind and the rain in your face: not effortless, maybe not even always that pleasant, in a conventional sense; but bracing, invigorating, and vital.

DAY TWENTY-FOUR

Scruffy hospitality

On finding connection in the flaws

'A perfectly kept house is the sign of a misspent life.'
— MARY RANDOLPH CARTER

J ack King, an Anglican priest from Tennessee, coined the phrase 'scruffy hospitality' in 2014. He and his wife enjoyed hosting friends for dinner, and they had a standard checklist they'd run through in the days and hours before guests were due to arrive: 'Select a menu, complete grocery shopping, mow the lawn, sweep the floors, run the vacuum, clean the playroom ... set the table, clean the play-room (again) and somehow, someway, pray all that happens before the doorbell rings.' Powering through the list made their home more inviting to visitors. But it also subtly dissuaded them from inviting more visitors, because it was so much work. Besides, King started to wonder, wasn't there something odd about putting so much effort into hiding the daily reality of their lives from the people they called their friends, or with whom they wanted to become friends? You might even define 'friendship' as the sort of connection between people that can't be imperiled by an unmown lawn or an unvacuumed carpet. And so King and his wife made an admirably imperfectionist decision: they'd start inviting friends to dine in their home as it was, and on whatever happened to be in the kitchen cupboards. As he put it later in a sermon:

> Scruffy hospitality means you're not waiting for everything in your house to be in order before you host and serve friends in your home. Scruffy hospitality means you hunger more for good conversation and serving a simple meal of what you have, not what you don't have. Scruffy hospitality means you're more interested in quality conversation than in the impression your home or lawn makes.

As a concept, scruffy hospitality would be valuable enough if all it conveyed was permission to put a little less effort into keeping a pristine home. But King was pointing to something deeper: being willing to let others see your life as it really is can be a positive act of generosity towards them, too. Even before encountering his work, I'd observed a strange contradiction in my own attitude to household mess. If

I noticed, say, crumbs underneath *our* fridge, or mail stacked inexplicably on top of *our* toaster, in the hours before guests arrived, I'd hurry to tidy things up. If I discovered an unflushed toilet – which happens, in homes with small kids – I'd breathe a sigh of relief that I'd discovered such a disastrous oversight in time. Yet if I noticed crumbs or stray letters while visiting friends, I'd feel obscurely privileged, as if I'd been granted the VIP access pass to their lives – so we must really be friends. Even an unflushed toilet would elicit no judgment from me. Why would it?

To put on an impressive show for visitors is to erect a facade, and there's nothing inherently wrong with that: some of us love the challenge of creating the most enchanting one we can. But the idea that such a facade is mandatory, if visitors are to be admitted to your life, must arise from the assumption that there's something incomplete or inadequate about your life the rest of the time. Since your visitors' home is presumably likewise usually a mess, it might even imply there's something wrong with their lives, too. No wonder calling off the whole performance forges a deeper bond. The moment I first see a friend's chaotic kitchen is like the moment in a blooper reel when two actors can't help breaking character and collapsing in laughter. Nominally, it shouldn't be happening, but it always feels delightfully real when it does.

Of course, the benefits of letting facades crumble aren't confined to dinner parties. Research into imposter syndrome provides another rich vein of examples. You might conclude that one good way to boost the confidence of people who feel like frauds at work would be to connect them with inspirational mentors. But when the sociologists Jessica Collett and Jade Avelis studied imposterism among entry-level academics, they discovered an unwelcome irony: mentoring schemes that paired young women with more experienced ones often made the younger scholars feel *more* insecure and inadequate, through negative comparison with their uber-accomplished elders. ('One said she suspected that her mentor was secretly Superwoman,' a report on the research explained. 'How could she ever live up to that example?') What seems to work much better is to encourage mentors to be more candid about their own failures and struggles: true confidence is kindled not by witnessing it in others, but by realizing you aren't alone in lacking it.

The Christian writer David Zahl refers to the view of humanity in which we approach each other on the assumption that everyone's imperfect and struggling, and prone to messing things up, as a 'low anthropology.' It's the opposite of a 'high anthropology,' in which we focus optimistically on the great things we expect from others and from ourselves – yet which all too often leads to anxiety, judgment, resentment and burnout. 'A high anthropology views people as defined by their best days and greatest achievements, their dreams and their aspirations,' Zahl writes. 'A low anthropology assumes a through line of heartache and self-doubt, [and] that the bulk of our mental energy is focused on subjects that would be embarrassing or even shameful if broadcast.' He illustrates the point by contrasting a famous 2005 commencement speech by Steve Jobs, in which the Apple founder urges his audience to search relentlessly for work they love,

and never to settle for less, with these words, from the essay-
ist Anne Lamott:

> Everyone is screwed up, broken, clingy, and scared, even the
> people who seem to have it more or less together. They are
> much more like you than you would believe. So try not to
> compare your insides to their outsides.

On the face of it, Jobs generously treats every one of his listeners as potential world-changers and billionaires, while
Lamott writes off the whole of humanity as a bunch of losers.
Yet there's real pressure in Jobs's supposedly inspiring exhor-
tation to keep striving to find your unique purpose – the
kind of pressure you could easily imagine inhibiting some
listeners from forging a bold path through life, instead of
encouraging them to do so, out of fear that they might not
measure up. By contrast, reading Lamott, 'you can feel your
shoulders unknot,' Zahl observes. The pressure is off. 'What
sounds insulting is actually liberating.'

And a liberation not just in the sense that you get to
relax, but also that you are freed to act. Knowing that I
needn't project a facade of flawless competence before I can
start daunting work or reach out to others – because I understand that everyone else has a similarly messy inner
world – leaves me far more likely to do so. Moreover, something about the fact that we're all in the same predicament
leaves me feeling supported by others in what I do, rather
than engaged in stress-inducing, zero-sum competition
against them. Our days become an extended exercise in

mutual scruffy hospitality – a dinner party in which we're all cooking for each other, and nobody's pretending it's anything fancier than spaghetti with tomato sauce, and the lack of pretense is exactly what makes it feel so convivial and full of life.

You can't hoard life

On letting the moments pass

'The nature of finite things as such is to have the seed
of passing away as their essential being: the hour of
their birth is the hour of their death.'

— G. W. F. HEGEL

A couple of years ago, my family and I moved from
Brooklyn to the North York Moors in northern
England, which means that very often in the early
mornings, carrying a flask of hot coffee, I get to stroll along
a lane with spectacular views across a valley to the heather-
topped ridge beyond. In winter, the pink light of sunrise
pours itself slowly over fields buried in snow; regularly, in
spring and summer, a barn owl swoops low across my path.
It's a magical landscape, and one that I've loved since
childhood.

You'd be surprised at how frequently I find a way to feel bad about this.

Or maybe you wouldn't, since this tendency to turn delightful experiences into stressful ones is rather widespread. Were I to put the stressful feeling into words, it might go roughly as follows: 'This is amazing! This is the kind of place in which I've always wanted to live, and the kind of thing I've always wanted to do in the early mornings – so I'd better make sure I'm getting the most out of it, and also, do whatever I can to make sure I can keep having this sort of experience forever, because it's slipping away already!' Mainly, though, the feeling I'm talking about isn't a matter of words. It's better described as a clenching or a gripping, an attempt to grasp hold of what's happening so as to mine it for as much value as possible, and somehow to claim ownership of it for myself. Needless to say, this is a suboptimal way to have an enjoyable experience.

Among spiritual traditions, Buddhism is uniquely insightful when it comes to this specific form of suffering – how we make ourselves more miserable than necessary, not just by railing against negative experiences we're having, or craving experiences we aren't having, but by trying too hard to hold on to good things that are happening exactly as we wanted them to. That's what's going on whenever you fail to savor a moment in nature, or with a newborn, or while eating an exceptional meal, because you're too focused on trying to savor it, or somehow extend it into the future. It's also what happens when you're too busy attempting to 'make memories' from an experience so as to be able to reflect upon it later – or, worse, to post pictures on social media. Another version of the same phenomenon occurs when you reach the end of a day on which you've been unusually successful in getting your work done, or sticking to your fitness routine, but then instead of thinking 'What a great day!' and luxuriating in your achievement, you find yourself thinking: 'Yes! Now *that's* the kind of day I'm aiming for, and now it's my job to make sure that this is merely the first of many such days to come!' Congratulations: you turned a potential source of easy delight into a cause of further stress.

In all these cases, in different ways, you're tightening around the experience in order to try to get more out of it – an additional level of enjoyment, motivation for future triumphs, or something else. Yet the reality, so easy to grasp on an intellectual level, is that it's detrimental to approach good experiences like this: they're for living, not holding on to. Spending your days trying to get experiences 'under your belt,' so as to maximize your collection of them, or to feel more confident about their future supply, means you never get to enjoy them properly because another agenda is at play. It's nice to collect memories, of course, but the way to do that isn't to go about trying to collect them. It's living them as fully as possible, so as to remember them vividly later.

'Perhaps all anxiety,' writes Sarah Manguso, 'might derive from a fixation on moments – an inability to accept life as ongoing.' Our attempt to grip on to fleeting experiences expresses the desire to store them up, use them for future purposes, freeze time in its tracks, or in some other way to resist the truth that *this is it*. And yet it follows from our finitude that the value of anything good that's happening now has to lie, at least in part, in our experience of it as it occurs, rather than in how we might co-opt it into our long-term project of trying to feel less finite. When I say I'd like to look out over the valley every morning 'forever,' I'm denying my finitude in a rather obvious way, because even if I were never to move house again and to live to the age of 130, there'd be no 'forever' about it. That would just be a few more decades of morning coffees, a less-than-invisible speck of time against the backdrop of the eons. All my clenching and grasping would have done precisely nothing to render the experience permanent.

Contrast these efforts to grab hold of experience with the spirit of the Japanese tea ceremony, in which fleetingness is understood not as a threat to what's unfolding, but as the source of its value. The exquisite precision of the ritual is intended to articulate and to honor the unrepeatable, unhoardable nature of the moment in which it occurs, as the nineteenth-century Japanese statesman Ii Naosuke explains:

> Great attention should be given to a tea gathering, which we can speak of as 'one time, one meeting' (*ichi-go, ichi-e*). Even though the host and guests may see each other often socially, one day's gathering can never be repeated exactly. Viewed this way, the meeting is indeed a once-in-a-lifetime occasion.

You can have a hundred tea ceremonies; you could even have all of them with the same people. But you can only have *that* ceremony, *that* cup of tea, once. Then that stretch of time evaporates forever. If it didn't – if, in defiance of all logic, it somehow persisted, so that you could return to it whenever you liked, for as long as you liked – it would be vastly less precious. The transience is the whole point.

On the days when I allow myself to move through life in this unclenched way, things are much more naturally enjoyable, because I'm not trying to make myself appreciate them, or self-consciously feel grateful for them. The less I'm trying to get something out of an experience, the more I find I can get into it, and the more I can be present for other people involved in it. This is not to say that life becomes a matter of unbroken good cheer; after all, it's *sad* that a beautiful moment arises then vanishes. But it's the flavor of sadness conveyed by the Japanese phrase *mono no aware*, a wistful pathos at the transience of things, the kind of poignant sadness that deepens an experience instead of detracting from it. The kind you feel once you're no longer grasping at the moment, thereby undermining your experience of it, but stepping more fully into it. Feeling yourself a part of it. Being it.

Inconceivable

On the solace of doubt

'In all the edifice of thought, I have found no category
on which to rest my head.'

— E. M. CIORAN

O ld Jewish joke:
The celebrated rabbi is on his deathbed. His
students are lined up in order of seniority to pay
their respects, awaiting his final words with bated breath.
Eventually, and with effort, the rabbi opens his eyes, then
addresses his most senior student. 'Life,' he declares, 'is a
river.' The student turns to the next most senior, and the message gets carried down the line: 'The rabbi says life is a river.'
'The rabbi says life is a river.' Only the most junior student,
the last to receive the words, is naive enough to venture a
question. 'But what does the rabbi mean, "life is a river"?' The

query comes back up the line, until the senior student, trembling at the audacity of questioning the master, manages to blurt it out. 'My rabbi, I'm sorry, but what do you *mean*, "life is a river"?'

The old man is moments from expiring. But for one last time, he opens his eyes, and regards the student in unblinking silence. Then he shrugs, and turns up his palms.

'All right,' he says. 'So it's *not* a river!'

At the risk of overanalyzing a joke, I think this one (which I encountered in this form via the academic Wilfred McClay) suggests that real wisdom doesn't lie in getting life figured out. It lies in grasping the sense in which you never will get it completely figured out.

This is not, though, the assumption on which we generally proceed through our days. When it comes to confronting the myriad problems large and small that life throws at us, we have a standard operating procedure for how we try to respond, one so fundamental it can be hard to perceive that it even is a procedure, or that there might be any alternative. It goes like this: first, you try to work out exactly what the hell is going on. Then and only then, once you're confident you've got a handle on the situation, you take action.

When the first part of this process – the figuring-out – goes too far, we call it 'analysis paralysis,' to describe the phenomenon of endlessly spinning your wheels in research and indecision. Yet few of us question the basic strategy itself. And when the strategy *fails* – when you can't seem to wrap your mind around what's happening to you, or in the wider world – the experience can be deeply disturbing. After all, it's genuinely hard to relax into life when you don't have a clue where your career might be headed, if your current relationship has a future, or what the rise of artificial intelligence might mean for your industry or for humanity's survival.

This is one more context in which it can be useful to try to imagine how things might have felt for a medieval peasant – or, really, for anyone at any time in history when people experienced life as radically more uncertain than today, yet were perhaps more clear-headed on the topic of human limitation. In those days, you couldn't ever have known with confidence what caused a famine or an outbreak of disease, nor felt reassured that a total eclipse didn't presage the end of the world. There'd be no way of telling if a family member's fever meant death or nothing much. Tradition and religion offered some broad explanations, and prescribed various rituals. But with certainty so hard to come by, it would never have occurred to you to make it a precondition for taking action that you should first attain a sound intellectual grasp of your specific situation. You'd have been accustomed to moving through life enveloped in uncertainty about almost everything that was going on, or what might happen next.

In this book, we've focused on what follows from the fact that we're so limited in how much we're able to do, how much time we get, and how much control we're able to exert. But we're constrained, as well, by an arguably even more basic intellectual limitation, which it's easy to lose sight of, in our era of so much information and advanced scientific knowledge. It's not a given, at any moment, that we'll even be able to understand what's happening, or what a reasonable response to it might be.

What if 'getting a handle on things' in this way wasn't

always necessary, though? What if, in fact, it was an obstacle to a fuller experience of life? The medieval comparison above originates with John Tarrant (who we met on Day Twenty-one, contemplating distraction and interruption) and he illustrates this argument with one of the most harrowing examples it's possible to imagine: that of a woman whose daughter died, and who found herself unable to wrap her mind around what had happened. Well-intentioned friends sought to help her recover a sense of meaning in life. But meaning was nowhere to be found; indeed, trying to find purpose after such a calamity only seemed to make things worse. What eventually brought a modicum of peace, and the first stirrings of forward motion, was the woman's reali-zation that a stable sense of meaning, and a clear grasp of what was happening to her, might be things that didn't need finding after all. Tarrant writes:

> She accepted that her life was now outside anything she had ever imagined, there was no reason for living, and, at the same time, there was no reason why she couldn't survive or feel joy ... She had to live merely for the sake of life, without justifications or achievements. She found that she was will-ing to do this. It also came to her that taking this path was generous to her daughter.

And if not needing to wrap your mind around what's hap-pening can provide a measure of solace and breathing-room in *that* situation, how might it help us get unstuck from the countless lesser difficulties that beset us all the time? Where could you take useful action on an important project, today, despite not really knowing how to proceed on it beyond that initial step? What issue in your life could you patch up – what relationship could you mend, what behavior could you alter – without fully grasping what went wrong in the first place? (Some people spend their whole lives trying to unpick the story of their childhoods, and sometimes it helps; but there's often a compulsive quality to the puzzling-out, and it can be better to give it a rest.) Perhaps most radically of all, what additional satisfaction could you take in your life, what fun could you have, once you glimpse a truth that must have come intuitively to premodern people, which is that since life is so inherently confusing and precarious, then joy, if it's ever to be found at all, is going to have to be found now, in the midst of the confusion and precariousness?

Those of us accustomed to relying on our intellects to power us through our days can get jumpy at the idea of relying on them less – of not always stopping to do research or think things through before acting on our intuitions. Yet over the course of humanity's history, it must have been far more common than not to feel adrift in a world of mysteries, obliged to proceed on the basis of blind hunches alone. So there need be no shame in the feeling that you don't yet fully understand the field you work in, or how to date, or be in a relationship, or be a parent. It doesn't mean something's wrong, and it doesn't mean you can't take constructive action – or, alternatively, relax – until all the answers are in. It just means that we're limited in our capacity to get a grip on our infinitely complex reality. It makes little sense to let that hold you back from living in it.

DAY TWENTY-SEVEN

C'est fait par du monde

On giving it a shot

'Life is like playing a violin solo in public and learning
the instrument as one goes on.'

— SAMUEL BUTLER

'But if we didn't aim for the impossible,' someone once
asked me at a public event, 'would we have made all
the scientific breakthroughs that we did? And what
about Steve Jobs, or Thomas Edison – didn't they do what
they did by reaching beyond their limits?' The question,
which I'm paraphrasing from memory, got at something that
understandably bothers us about embracing limitation. Isn't
it essential precisely to refuse to embrace limitation, so as to
surpass the status quo, to demolish the assumption that life
as we know it is as good as we should ever expect it to get?

The answer, I think, is mainly that we confuse two

different meanings of the word 'impossible.' When I call something impossible in this book, I straightforwardly mean that it can't be done, according to the most fundamental laws that govern humans in space and time. You can't be in two places at once; you don't have unlimited time; you can't know for certain what the future holds; you can't render yourself so efficient that no incoming volume of work could ever overwhelm you. (I suppose I must concede that developments on the frontiers of technology, like duplicating and uploading a human consciousness, might one day change even some of these. But let's put that aside for now.) My questioner was referring to achievements of the kind that once seemed astounding – the eradication of smallpox, perhaps, or the invention of the light bulb, or at least the iPhone – and he was correct that humanity needs people unwilling to write off such visions as impossible. But the relationship between the two kinds of 'impossible' is actually an inverse one. In other words, the more willing you are wholeheartedly to acknowledge the hard limitations of human finitude, the easier it gets to do what others might dismiss as impossible. Once you stop struggling to get on top of everything, to stay in absolute control, or to make everything perfect, you're rewarded with the time, energy and psychological freedom to accomplish the most of which anyone could be capable.

The best way I've ever seen this encapsulated was in a phrase that an anonymous internet poster attributed to their French-Canadian grandmother, who could apparently be relied upon to deliver it whenever a family member expressed overawed admiration for a dazzling work of art or a stunning technological advance: 'C'est fait par du monde.' Roughly:

'People did that.' It's a truth that can't be disputed: if something exists in reality, and it wasn't already a part of the natural environment, then it must have been made by one or more flawed and finite people – not one of whom had any greater ability to overcome their built-in human limitations than you. The greatest novel you ever read? A person wrote it. The most effective philanthropic organization on the planet? Just people. The Golden Gate Bridge, the Pyramids at Giza, and the Palace of Versailles? More people. And the corollary, of course, is that if people did all that, there's no inherent reason why you couldn't also do, or contribute to, astounding things as well.

Naturally, it doesn't follow that you can do every specific thing you might put your mind to. Flawed and finite people fly airliners and perform open-heart surgery every day, yet it remains the case that almost all of us should refrain from seeking to emulate them. And talent is at least partly inborn: I doubt there's any form of educational intervention, even beginning at birth and costing millions, that could have led to my winning the Fields Medal in mathematics. Economic circumstances impose further hard limits on what many get the chance to accomplish. Still, the point stands: nothing that anyone has ever done required superhuman capacities in order to do it.

Which brings me to L. Ron Hubbard, the founder of Scientology, and an observation I'm concerned may come across as unduly admiring of the man. So let's get the obvious caveats out of the way: Scientology has been heavily criticized, and Hubbard, at least on the evidence of Lawrence Wright's 2013 book *Going Clear*, was a notorious philanderer, violent narcissist, and fabulist. (One example: he liked to tell stories of torpedoing Japanese submarines as captain of a US Navy ship during the Second World War, but, on Wright's account, was probably really firing at nothing, or at logs floating by in the ocean.) The only trait of Hubbard's that might qualify as a compliment is this: he decided he was going to start a religion, and he just went for it. The outlandishness or difficulty of the task seems never to have struck him as an obstacle. Watching old archive footage of the lectures he delivered in England in the 1960s, before going on the run from the authorities, it seems as though he is making Scientology up. I don't just mean that Hubbard's wild tales of intergalactic rulers trapping people in volcanoes then blowing them up with hydrogen bombs emerged from his imagination, which they obviously did. My (unprovable) theory is that he was literally making things up as he went along. 'I remember one time, about 12 trillion years ago,' begins one of countless anecdotes, to which he'd apparently given zero prior thought. He didn't just invent a religion. He *improvised* one. Badly. And it worked! That's confidence – even if put to unfortunate use.

The lesson, to reiterate, isn't that you ought to start a religion. It's that if that old windbag can do so, you can probably have a go at launching any project about which you've been experiencing self-doubt – and that there's no reason why you can't be the one to make a fortune, or a long-lasting difference to the world, as a result. Likewise, if you've been thinking of making a radical change in your life – traveling the world in midlife, say, or educating your kids outside the school system – there's a solid chance you can scrabble together the resources and figure out a way. You won't feel like you know what you're doing. But nobody ever does; that's just how it is for finite humans, attempting new things. The main difference between those who accomplish great things anyway and those who don't is that the former don't mind not knowing. They were not less flawed or finite than you. Everything they ever did was done by people.

DAY TWENTY-EIGHT

What matters

On finding your way

'It was said of Rabbi Simcha Bunim that he carried
two slips of paper, one in each pocket. On one he
wrote: *Bishvili nivra ha'olam* – "For my sake the world
was created." On the other he wrote: *V'anokhi afar
v'aefer* – "I am but dust and ashes." He would take out
each slip of paper as necessary, as a reminder to
himself.'

— TOBA SPITZER

I n his *Meditations*, Marcus Aurelius recommends a
mental exercise we might today call 'zooming out':
whenever you're feeling anxious or overwhelmed – or,
alternatively, too full of yourself – try expanding your awareness of reality from your small patch of ground to the world

as a whole. This will put things in perspective. Even more powerfully, consider your moment in time against the backdrop of the eons:

> Often think of the rapidity with which things pass by and disappear ... For substance is like a river in continual flow, and the activities of things are in constant change, and the causes work in infinite varieties; and there is hardly anything which stands still. And consider this which is near to thee, this boundless abyss of the past and of the future in which all things disappear. How then is he not a fool who is puffed up with such things or plagued about them and makes himself miserable? For they vex him only for a time, and a short time.

I'm always taken aback by the relaxation that floods through me when I'm reminded of my almost complete lack of importance in the scheme of things. One might expect to find such reflections depressing or demotivating. But I experience them as liberating; my shoulders drop, and I'm able to exhale. The truth, as one spiritual teacher puts it, is that reality doesn't need me to help operate it. It carries on fine regardless. Which is obvious – except that the level of stress we generally attach to our efforts to resolve our little problems would seem to imply otherwise.

This raises a troubling question, though. If nothing any of us does has any significance, provided you zoom out far enough, what's the point of doing anything?

We have reached the end of this journey into finitude. Over the last four weeks, we've confronted what it means to accept that there will always be too much to do, and that the future will always be out of our control. We've explored the role of bold, imperfect action at the core of a fulfilling finite existence; how it's often wisest to get out of the way and let reality happen; and what's involved in showing up, as fully as possible, for a limited human life. Yet throughout it all, I've shirked what some might view as my one job in a book like this: explaining which things – which projects, activities, relationships and experiences – make for the most meaningful life. The reason is that in your case, I haven't much of a clue – and I'm certain it's intrinsic to the value of any answer that we each arrive at it ourselves. There are few more reliable ways to destroy any feelings of meaning, or the sense of vibrancy and aliveness that Hartmut Rosa calls resonance, than by attempting to implement some book's list of Fulfilling Ways to Live. Besides, it's always the same list: nurture your relationships, pursue challenging goals, spend time in nature, and make room for fun. You knew that already. If following a list was all it took, we'd have solved the challenge of human happiness long ago.

And so I won't be concluding here by revealing the meaning of life. But I do have thoughts.

The first is that it simply need not follow, from our cosmic insignificance as individuals, that our actions don't matter. The idea that things only count if they count on the vastest scale is one more expression of our discomfort with finitude: accepting that they might count only transiently, or locally, requires us to face our limitations and our mortality. And so to avoid that unpleasantness, as the philosopher Iddo Landau has explained, we gravitate towards an unnecessarily grandiose standard of what matters – then get demoralized when our achievements don't make the grade. We feel pressured to do something extraordinary with our lives, or to an extraordinary standard of merit, or in a way that's applauded by an extraordinary number of people – even though it's true by definition that only a few people can ever be extraordinary in any given domain. (If we could all stand out from the crowd, there'd be no crowd from which to stand out.) Why shouldn't an anonymous career spent quietly helping a few people get to qualify as a meaningful way to spend one's time? Why shouldn't an absorbing conversation, an act of kindness, or an exhilarating hike get to count? Why adopt a definition that rules such things out?

It can be enlightening, also, to notice when our intellectual theories about what matters crumble in the face of an intuitive sense that what we're doing is meaningful, theories be damned. The writer Charles Eisenstein tells the story of a friend, a prominent activist, who largely abandoned his public work to care for his 95-year-old mother-in-law. Eisenstein envisions the blowback he might have received from fellow activists: How could he justify that use of his time, with the world in such peril? I've seen similar arguments made by people who fear that artificial intelligence will eradicate humanity: if there's even a modest chance that's true, how could anyone spend their finite time on anything else? The answer has to be that sometimes you just know you're doing something that matters. Far from using utilitarian calculations to try to squelch that felt sense, I think we have an obligation to it. It may embody more wisdom than our finite reasoning can grasp. I'm comfortable saying that if it follows from any given value system that, say, caring for a 95-year-old who needs help is a waste of your time, then the problem lies with the value system – not with the act of care.

There is one further assumption we tend not to question when contemplating what matters, which is the subtle notion that we're fundamentally separate from the rest of reality. (As we saw on Day Four, we often use productivity to try to earn back the right to belong.) On this account, we come into the world as solitary individuals, and it's as solitary individuals, in the end, that we must address the challenge of using our time – even if we decide to prioritize relationships, political solidarity, or community-building. Yet, as the Zen philosopher Alan Watts liked to point out, it makes just as much sense to say that we come out of the world: that in the same way a tree blossoms, the universe 'peoples.' We are expressions of it. Our very being is inseparable from our context, or as Thich Nhat Hanh puts it, we 'inter-are'; my existence would be wholly impossible without countless people and things I standardly think of as separate from myself. Perhaps the ultimate expression of our finitude is the fact that we are irrevocably *of* the world, whether we like it or not. If so, then maybe our responsibility isn't to get our arms around it, nor to justify ourselves before it, but to embody as completely as possible the momentary expression of it that we are.

From this perspective, it makes no sense to judge your activities by the unreachable standards of a god, nor to fault yourself for having only a minuscule impact on the whole. There's no reason to see 'getting on top of things' as the target of your endeavors in the first place – and still less to imagine that you might manage to obtain a sense of security regarding the crises engulfing the planet, which will doubtless continue to engulf it long after you're gone. Instead, you get to pour yourself into tasks that matter for no other reason than that nothing could be more enlivening, or more true to the situation in which you find yourself. You get to proceed in the splendidly imperfectionist spirit of the eco-philosopher Derrick Jensen, who says: 'The good thing about everything being so fucked up is that no matter where you look, there is great work to be done.'

You might easily never have been born, but fate granted you the opportunity to get stuck into the mess you see around you, whatever it is. You are here. This is it. You don't much matter – yet you matter as much as anyone ever did. The river of time flows inexorably on; amazingly, confoundingly, marvelously, we get the brief chance to go kayaking in it.

EPILOGUE

Imperfectly onward

'There was the cat, asleep. He ordered a cup of coffee, slowly stirred the sugar, sipped it (this pleasure had been denied him in the clinic), and thought, as he smoothed the cat's black coat, that this contact was an illusion and that the two beings, man and cat, were as good as separated by a glass, for man lives in time, in succession, while the magical animal lives in the present, in the eternity of the instant.'

— JORGE LUIS BORGES

If you've accompanied me this far, I trust it won't come as a devastating shock to learn that, notwithstanding this book's subtitle, no one should expect to fully embrace their limits, confront their mortality and find psychological freedom in a mere four weeks. Self-help promises such as 'six

159

weeks to six-pack abs' or 'thirty days to a stress-free you' may get broken far more often than they're kept, but when it comes to imperfectionism, it's worse, because by definition the journey is never complete. Were I to suggest that completing it might be possible, I'd simply be fueling the same old fantasy of sorting your life out, in a marginally more sophisticated way. The truth is that you'll never be certain that an unmeetable challenge or regrettable choice isn't just around the next corner, or that the projects I hope you're newly energized to dig into will meet with success. The spiritual teacher Joan Tollifson calls our yearning for finality 'the compulsion to closure,' a sort of tic, eminently forgivable, but which the world can never satisfy – and which we might gradually therefore learn to relax, so as to more wholeheartedly take our place in, and as part of, the unending flow of reality.

Besides the fact that you shouldn't expect to transform your life in four weeks, it can be startlingly liberating to consider that in some domains, you might never change it at all – and that that's fine. The psychotherapist Bruce Tift suggests the following reflection: pick the trait that bothers you the most about yourself or your life – your tendency to procrastinate or get distracted, perhaps, or your short fuse, or your proneness to gloomy moods – and then ask yourself what it feels like to imagine that some version of it might dog you to the end of your days. What if I'll always have anxious reactions – the clench in the stomach, the sharp intake of breath – to minor events that don't warrant them? My first response is to feel crestfallen; but soon thereafter comes relief. I get to give up on that futile struggle, which means I needn't wait for it to be won before diving into reality. Maybe I never needed to change in order to justify my existence. Maybe I was always up to the task of building a meaningful life.

On a closely related point: if you've found this book in any way inspiring, you may be tempted, at this juncture, to resolve to make a fresh start, to declare that from today – or next week, once you've got various urgent business out of the way – you'll do everything differently forever. This is an urge worth resisting: it's a perfectionistic attitude towards imperfectionism, and a recipe for disappointment. Our limitations make fresh starts impossible: you are already here, in time, shaped by everything that came before this moment, and with whatever personality, resources and challenges you find yourself to have. Screwing up your willpower and insisting you're leaving that all behind is unlikely to change much. On the other hand, more fully accepting that you are who you are, and where you are, might change a lot, by permitting you to abandon the dream of a fresh start and actually do one thing today that truly matters, and that makes life resonate once more.

It would be nice not to have to bother with any of this, of course. There's something to be envied in the inner life of the cat, as imagined by Borges: like most non-human animals, at least as far as we know, it lives only here and now, with no capacity to contemplate any other possibility. Humans get to accomplish much more than cats, and probably to experience a far richer panoply of emotions. But the price we must pay is facing hard truths: that we'll die; that life unfolds one moment after another; that each moment represents a choice among competing ways of spending our time, so that agonizing choices, and the sacrifice of alternative worthy paths, are inevitable; and that we'll never achieve emotional invulnerability, or a sense of full control.

As an imperfectionist, you don't have to pretend this situation is without its poignancy, its seasons of grief, its spells of loneliness, confusion or despair. But you no longer fight as hard as you once did to persuade yourself this isn't the way things are, or that human existence ought to be otherwise. Instead, you choose to put down that impossible burden – and to keep on putting it down when you realize, as you frequently will, that you've inadvertently picked it up again. And so you move forward into life with greater vigor, a more peaceful mind, more openness to others, and, on your better days, the exhilaration that comes from savoring reality's bracing air.

Acknowledgments

Increasingly it seems to me that the process of writing a book isn't about deciding what you want it to be, but attempting to figure out what *it* wants to be. I still can't quite believe my good fortune when it comes to the people with whom I get to do this. This project was nourished into life by a series of conversations with the wise and spirited Robin Parmiter, and through many communications with readers of my email newsletter: thank you. It would have gone nowhere without my superb agents Claire Conrad and Melissa Flashman, who are unrivaled at bridging the gap between ideas and making things real in the world. I had the great pleasure of collaborating once more with Stuart Williams at The Bodley Head and Eric Chinski at Farrar, Straus and Giroux: my writing is better for their editorial insights and advice, their generous attention, and their friendly but firm insistence on clarifying my ideas and arguments. The creativity and expertise of many of their colleagues also proved indispensable. Much thanks also to Emma Brockes, Merope Mills, and Rachael Parmiter.

I am luckiest of all for the love, friendship, and wisdom of Heather Chaplin, who made real sacrifices for this book, and for Rowan Burkeman, who is simply fantastic. They're my best reminders of what really matters, and of the fact that life is something to delight in, not merely to be dealt with. Any true aliveness in these pages is down to them as much as to me.

Further Reading

Week One: Being Finite

The notion that our real problem isn't being finite but struggling to *escape* the condition of being finite is a recurring motif in Zen writing; I recommend Charlotte Joko Beck's bracing collection *Nothing Special: Living Zen.* Joan Tollifson approaches the topic from a more eclectic perspective in her wonderfully titled *Death: The End of Self-Improvement,* while Kelly Kapic investigates its relevance for Christians in *You're Only Human: How Your Limits Reflect God's Design and Why That's Good News.* (Jordan Raynor's *Redeeming Your Time* is another Christian book, full of finitude-embracing productivity tips that don't depend on any particular religious belief.) If you're the sort of person who enjoys cold showers and punishing triathlons, you might try exploring Martin Heidegger's *Being and Time*: Joan Stambaugh's translation is the least unreadable one, though I also relied on Richard Polt's *Heidegger: An Introduction* and Hubert Dreyfus's lectures, available on YouTube. The idea that you're free to do what you like, so long as you're willing to face the consequences, comes from Sheldon Kopp's delightful book *If You Meet the Buddha on the Road, Kill Him!: The Pilgrimage of Psychotherapy Patients* – and the existentialist view that meaning arises through taking responsibility for your actions underpins Sara Kuburic's thoughtful self-help book *It's on Me: Embrace Hard Truths, Discover Your Self and Change Your Life*. (For the best introduction to the milieu and message of the existentialists, read Sarah Bakewell's *At the Existentialist Café: Freedom, Being and Apricot Cocktails*.) Robert Saltzman's book *The Ten Thousand Things* is the source of his quoted observations on our inability to control the future, and is full of similarly pithy, no-nonsense insights into the vulnerability of our situation.

Week Two: Taking Action

Recommending books on how to take action is a dangerous game, because any such pointers are liable to being used as an excuse to read yet another book on taking action, instead of taking it. That said, titles on the topic that have genuinely helped trigger action in my own life include Steve Chandler's *Time Warrior* and Gregg Krech's *The Art of Taking Action: Lessons from Japanese Psychology*. Many of the principles of finitude-embracing productivity are encapsulated in the time management system known as Kanban, which is lucidly outlined in *Personal Kanban: Mapping Work/Navigating Life* by

Jim Benson and Tonianne DeMaria; there are also overlaps with Cal Newport's advice on dividing your projects into 'active' and 'waiting to be active,' which is one of the gems in his book *Slow Productivity: The Lost Art of Accomplishment Without Burnout*. Zen and time management come together in Paul Loomans's *Time Surfing: The Zen Approach to Keeping Time on Your Side*, which contains a remarkable amount of wisdom for such a short book; and anyone paralyzed with anxiety about a daunting project should read Virginia Valian's essay 'Learning to Work,' which she makes available on her website, virginiavalian.org. Alex Soojung-Kim Pang's *Rest: Why You Get More Done When You Work Less* makes good on the promise of its subtitle, and should convince you that impressive output requires no superhuman investment of time. For puzzling out what you ought to be doing with your time – and for finding solace and clarity in periods of confusion or despair – I unequivocally recommend the work of James Hollis. My introduction to his writing was *Finding Meaning in the Second Half of Life: How to Finally, Really Grow Up*.

Week Three: Letting Go

On the art of letting life happen, the text of all texts is, of course, the *Tao Te Ching* by Laozi – or probably in fact by some assemblage of ancient authors now collectively referred to as Laozi, 'the Old Master.' I recommend the translation by Gia-fu Feng and Jane English, accompanied by English's exhilarating photographs. There's nothing difficult about it (or about life, Laozi might add, and that's the whole point).

But the Taoist philosophy of 'effortless action,' the diametric opposite of much contemporary life advice, is also usefully explored in three more modern and somewhat less poetical books: *Effortless Living: Wu-Wei and the Spontaneous State of Natural Harmony* by Jason Gregory, Edward Slingerland's *Trying Not to Try: The Art and Science of Spontaneity*, and *Tao: The Watercourse Way* by Alan Watts. Iddo Landau's discussion of the 'reverse golden rule,' and the added cruelty we reserve for when we're talking to ourselves, comes from his book *Finding Meaning in an Imperfect World*, which is a storehouse of insights on making a meaningful life from the situation in which we find ourselves. The best practical recent words on self-acceptance as a path to accomplishing good things are in Elizabeth Gilbert's *Big Magic: Creative Living Beyond Fear*. Hartmut Rosa's long book with a short title, *Resonance*, and his short book with a long one, *The Uncontrollability of the World*, were both essential for me in writing this one, and I think his analysis of what makes modern life so strangely unfulfilling for so many people deserves your attention. Stephen Lloyd Webber's book *Deep Freewriting: How to Masterfully Navigate the Creative Flow* conveys a good feel for the profound psychological benefits of the practice. One day, I'll try the twenty-four-hour freewriting marathon he recommends.

Week Four: Showing Up

The idea that human finitude makes it ultimately absurd to live entirely for the benefit of our future selves is powerfully driven home in Dean Rickles's book *Life is Short: An*

Appropriately Brief Guide to Making It More Meaningful. And Sheryl Paul explores a complementary perspective – what our anxiety has to teach us about living more fully now – in *The Wisdom of Anxiety: How Worry and Intrusive Thoughts Are Gifts to Help You Heal.* Byung-Chul Han's *Vita Contemplativa: In Praise of Inactivity* pinpoints the frenetic and avoidant nature of so much of what passes for productivity, while Elizabeth Oldfield's book *Fully Alive: Tending to the Soul in Turbulent Times* is a strikingly wise and companionable account of what a more wholehearted life entails. Once again, for me, the Zen tradition has proved indispensable in actually feeling what it means to step more fully into present reality; I'll mention here above all *Opening the Hand of Thought: Foundations of Zen Buddhist Practice* by Kōshō Uchiyama; Shinshu Roberts's *Being-Time: A Practitioner's Guide to Dogen's Shobogenzo Uji*; and the works of John Tarrant, chiefly *Bring Me the Rhinoceros: And Other Zen Koans That Will Save Your Life.* David Zahl's *Low Anthropology: The Unlikely Key to a Gracious View of Others (and Yourself)* is a liberating guide to living finitely and forgivingly together. There are surely countless other eminently worthwhile books on all of these topics. If only there were time to read them all.

Index of Afflictions

Refer to this alphabetical catalogue of common troubles to find chapters especially relevant to each.

Analysis paralysis
   You need only face the consequences: On paying the price 14
   Decision-hunting: On choosing a path through the woods 45
   Set a quantity goal: On firing your inner quality controller 108
Anger
   Develop a taste for problems: On never reaching the trouble-free
      phase 75
   What's an interruption, anyway?: On the importance of staying
      distractible 113
Anxiety
   Against productivity debt: On the power of a 'done list' 20
   Let the future be the future: On crossing bridges when you come to
      them 37
   Allow other people their problems: On minding your own
      business 97

Avoidance

Kayaks and superyachts: On actually doing things 9

Just go to the shed: On befriending what you fear 60

Busyness

It's worse than you think: On the liberation of defeat 3

Against productivity debt: On the power of a 'done list' 20

Too much information: On the art of reading and not reading 26

How to start from sanity: On paying yourself first 127

Dauntedness

You need only face the consequences: On paying the price 14

You can't care about everything: On staying sane when the world's a mess 31

Just go to the shed: On befriending what you fear 60

What if this were easy?: On the false allure of effort 81

Demotivation

Decision-hunting: On choosing a path through the woods 45

What if this were easy?: On the false allure of effort 81

C'est fait par du monde: On giving it a shot 148

Despair in general

It's worse than you think: On the liberation of defeat 3

Look for the life task: On what reality wants 55

Despair at the state of the world

You can't care about everything: On staying sane when the world's a mess 31

Directionlessness

Look for the life task: On what reality wants 55

What matters: On finding your way 153

Disempowerment

You need only face the consequences: On paying the price 14

You can't care about everything: On staying sane when the world's a mess 31

What if this were easy?: On the false allure of effort 81

Disengagement

Stop being so kind to Future You: On entering time and space completely 121

You can't hoard life: On letting the moments pass 138

Distraction

Too much information: On the art of reading and not reading 26

Three hours: On finding focus in the chaos 70

What's an interruption, anyway?: On the importance of staying distractible 113

Fear of the future

You can't care about everything: On staying sane when the world's a mess 31

Let the future be the future: On crossing bridges when you come to them 37

Fear of taking action

Decision-hunting: On choosing a path through the woods 45

Just go to the shed: On befriending what you fear 60

What if this were easy?: On the false allure of effort 81

Guilt

You need only face the consequences: On paying the price 14

Against productivity debt: On the power of a 'done list' 20

The reverse golden rule: On not being your own worst enemy 87

Don't stand in generosity's way: On the futility of 'becoming a better person' 93

Hurry

Against productivity debt: On the power of a 'done list' 20

Let the future be the future: On crossing bridges when you come to them 37

How to start from sanity: On paying yourself first 127

Imposter syndrome

It's worse than you think: On the liberation of defeat 3

The reverse golden rule: On not being your own worst enemy 87

Scruffy hospitality: On finding connection in the flaws 132

Inconsistency

Rules that serve life: On doing things dailyish 65

Indecision

You need only face the consequences: On paying the price 14

Decision-hunting: On choosing a path through the woods 45

Look for the life task: On what reality wants 55

Information overload

Too much information: On the art of reading and not reading 26

Insecurity

Against productivity debt: On the power of a 'done list' 20

Let the future be the future: On crossing bridges when you come to them 37

Interruptions

What's an interruption, anyway?: On the importance of staying distractible 113

Irritability

Develop a taste for problems: On never reaching the trouble-free phase 75

What's an interruption, anyway? On the importance of staying distractible 113

Lifelessness

A good time or a good story: On the upsides of unpredictability 102

Stop being so kind to Future You: On entering time and space completely 121

You can't hoard life: On letting the moments pass 138

Loneliness

What's an interruption, anyway?: On the importance of staying distractible 113

Scruffy hospitality: On finding connection in the flaws 132

Meaninglessness

    Look for the life task: On what reality wants 55

    Inconceivable: On the solace of doubt 143

    What matters: On finding your way 153

Mean-spiritedness

    Don't stand in generosity's way: On the futility of 'becoming a better person' 93

Need for control

    It's worse than you think: On the liberation of defeat 3

    Three hours: On finding focus in the chaos 70

    A good time or a good story: On the upsides of unpredictability 102

Nonproductivity

    Against productivity debt: On the power of a 'done list' 20

    Decision-hunting: On choosing a path through the woods 45

    Rules that serve life: On doing things dailyish 65

    Three hours: On finding focus in the chaos 70

Overwhelm at the difficulty of challenges *see* Dauntedness

Overwhelm at the quantity of tasks *see* Busyness

Perfectionism

    It's worse than you think: On the liberation of defeat 3

    Kayaks and superyachts: On actually doing things 9

    Rules that serve life: On doing things dailyish 65

    The reverse golden rule: On not being your own worst enemy 87

    Set a quantity goal: On firing your inner quality controller 108

Pessimism

    It's worse than you think: On the liberation of defeat 3

    You can't care about everything: On staying sane when the world's a mess 31

    C'est fait par du monde: On giving it a shot 148

Powerlessness *see* Disempowerment

Problems in general

You need only face the consequences: On paying the price 14

Just go to the shed: On befriending what you fear 60

Develop a taste for problems: On never reaching the trouble-free phase 75

Procrastination

Kayaks and superyachts: On actually doing things 9

Decision-hunting: On choosing a path through the woods 45

Just go to the shed: On befriending what you fear 60

Putting things off

Kayaks and superyachts: On actually doing things 9

Stop being so kind to Future You: On entering time and space completely 121

How to start from sanity: On paying yourself first 127

Regret

Decision-hunting: On choosing a path through the woods 45

A good time or a good story: On the upsides of unpredictability 102

You can't hoard life: On letting the moments pass 138

Relationship troubles

It's worse than you think: On the liberation of defeat 3

You need only face the consequences: On paying the price 14

Allow other people their problems: On minding your own business 97

Rush *see* Hurry

Sadness in general

You can't care about everything: On staying sane when the world's a mess 31

The reverse golden rule: On not being your own worst enemy 87

Sadness at the transience of life

You can't hoard life: On letting the moments pass 138

What matters: On finding your way 153

Self-criticism
  Against productivity debt: On the power of a 'done list' 20
  The reverse golden rule: On not being your own worst enemy 87
  Stop being so kind to Future You: On entering time and space completely 121

Timidity
  C'est fait par du monde: On giving it a shot 148

Unfinished business
  Finish things: On the magic of completion 51
  Just go to the shed: On befriending what you fear 60

Worry about the future *see* Fear of the future
Worry about other people's opinions
  You need only face the consequences: On paying the price 14
  Allow other people their problems: On minding your own business 97
  Scruffy hospitality: On finding connection in the flaws 132
Writers' block
  It's worse than you think: On the liberation of defeat 3
  Three hours: On finding focus in the chaos 70
  Set a quantity goal: On firing your inner quality controller 108

A NOTE ABOUT THE AUTHOR

Oliver Burkeman worked for many years at *The Guardian*, where he wrote a popular weekly column on psychology, "This Column Will Change Your Life." His books include the *New York Times* bestseller *Four Thousand Weeks: Time Management for Mortals* and *The Antidote: Happiness for People Who Can't Stand Positive Thinking*.

You can subscribe to Oliver Burkeman's email newsletter, *The Imperfectionist*, at oliverburkeman.com.